TEACH YOURSELF BOOKS

THE PIANO

TEACH YOURSELF BOOKS

THE PIANO

King Palmer
Associate of the Royal Academy of Music

Long-renowned as *the* authoritative source for self-guided learning – with more than 30 million copies sold worldwide – the *Teach Yourself* series includes over 200 titles in the fields of languages, crafts, hobbies, sports, and other leisure activities.

This edition was first published in 1992 by NTC Publishing Group, 4255 West Touhy Avenue, Lincolnwood (Chicago), Illinois 60646 – 1975 U.S.A. Originally published by Hodder and Stoughton Ltd.

Printed in England by Clays Ltd, St Ives plc.

Contents

Preface

Since I first wrote *The Piano* for this series it has been reprinted many times but only small revisions have been possible, and I have long felt that I should like to write an entirely new book which would take into account new ideas about piano playing, and my own continuing thoughts and experiences as a teacher and musician. This book has now been completely rewritten and reset.

Quite a few people have told me that they have learned to play the piano with the help of my book, but in fairness I have not heard them play. I think, however, that this book should be able to impart sufficient knowledge to enable someone to *enjoy* playing the piano, and perhaps to give enjoyment to others. It may even be the means of revealing some hitherto undiscovered talent, so that the reader will be persuaded to take piano lessons from an experienced teacher.

Of the many adults who do have a real desire to play, some, who have studied piano playing at any earlier period of their lives, would like to remind themselves of things they have almost ceased to remember; but, like others who have never played at all, they may wonder how much progress they are likely to make. I think that, given the desire and will to learn, it is never too late to start. Of course if one is older it may take longer but then one may have a little more time to spare.

I hope that would-be pianists who read this book will find it of help in one way or another. Perhaps, also, it may sometimes help piano students when they are trying to resolve problems of theory and technique which present themselves in their teacher's absence.

In preparing this book I have been greatly encouraged by the interest shown by many of my friends. I am especially grateful to Harold Britton and Brian Black for reading the whole book in typescript, and for offering many helpful comments and suggestions; and to Helena O'Connell for patient and thoughtful help in preparing the manuscript for press.

Notes on American usage

1 American 'cancel' = British 'natural' (after sharp or flat sign).

2 There is a distinction between British and American usage of the words 'tone' and 'note'. In British usage 'tone' usually means either (a) the interval of a major second (i.e. two semitones); or (b) the quality of a musical sound; and 'note' either (a) the actual written or printed sign which represents the pitch and duration of a musical sound; or (b) an actual sound of musical pitch; or (c) the finger-key of a piano, organ, etc. In American usage 'tone' (from the German 'ton') may be used to describe an actual sound of musical pitch, whereas 'note' is usually reserved for the written or printed sign. Thus 'three notes higher' (British) becomes 'three tones higher' (American).

3 Distinctions between British and American names of the varieties of notes and rests will be found on pages 25 and 30.

4 'Measure', an old English term, is used in America as the equivalent of British 'bar'; in America, 'bar' is often reserved for British 'bar-line' (see page 20).

5 *Degrees of the scale.* British 'submediant' is sometimes American 'superdominant'; sometimes, also, British 'leading note' becomes American 'subtonic' or 'leading tone'.

1

How to Use This Book

Perhaps you have never played the piano, and have just opened this book. Or perhaps you did play long ago, and have almost forgotten how. If you came to me for a first lesson, the situation would be rather different. I could ask whether you had a musical background, if you could read music, why you wanted to play the piano, what music you had heard and enjoyed. I could even invite you to try a few aural tests, which would give me some idea of your musical ability.

But whether you choose to take lessons from a teacher or to learn what you can from a book (or perhaps even from both) there are certain objects and skills that you will need before you can make a start. The first is a piano to play on and, unless you already possess one, or have access to one for regular practice, your first concern will be to obtain a suitable instrument. This is considered in Chapter 2, which also discusses ways of looking after a piano, and gives a brief description of how the instrument works.

Then, if you are not already able to read music, you will need to learn some theory – about notes, time, scale formation, and so on. Large doses of theory can be indigestible, so I have introduced it gradually, in four chapters which can be studied separately, so, if you wish, you will be able to start playing something simple at an early stage.

When you can read music you will need some to play from. Music can be borrowed from some public libraries, but if you are a beginner you should have a small basic collection of your own. It need not be expensive, and could comprise these items:

A book of scales

Scale books published by the Associated Board are suitable; the Grade Four book would last a beginner a long time.

A book of easy studies

Either of these would be suitable:

Graded Pianoforte Studies, Preliminary, 1st and 2nd Series (Associated Board).

Preliminary Exercises for Piano, Hanon, ed. John Thompson (Chappell).

A book of easy pieces

A Keyboard Anthology, Book One, 1st, 2nd and 3rd Series (Associated Board).

Classics to Moderns, Book One (Yorktown Music Press).

A book of aural tests

Part One (Associated Board).

A book of music paper

Writing music is an important part of learning it, so you will need this. Some of the music examples in this book are printed along, rather than across the page. It is recommended that those which are to be played should be copied in to a book of music paper; this will provide you with a valuable lesson in note-reading and also enable you to read the music from the piano.

These books will probably last you for a year or so, unless you are able to put in a considerable amount of practice, and so make exceptional progress. After that you can, if you wish, continue with studies and pieces in the same series, but in a higher grade. By this time, however, you will probably be able to make suitable choices on your own, either to buy, or to borrow. If you would like special music for sight-reading, the *Read and Play Series* (Grade One) by Thomas A. Johnston (Hinrichsen) is useful. If you have had previous experience of piano playing, you will be able to make a start with pieces and studies of a higher grade, and to make appropriate choices accordingly.

In writing this book I have, as far as possible, arranged the chapters progressively, but learning is a personal undertaking, and it is not really possible to lay down hard and fast rules. I suggest, therefore, that first you should read through the entire book (except for the Demonstration Lessons) fairly rapidly. After this, study each chapter in depth, with cross-references to other chapters, and to the index and glossary of terms, whenever necessary. Most chapters can be studied in any order you wish, but whenever possible they should be applied to music which you are practising. The four chapters on Theory of Piano Music should be studied in order, but they need not be taken all together. As soon as you feel confident to tackle a simple study or piece you should do so. But it is important that you should check your knowledge of theory by answering the Self-Testing Questions, which you will find at the end of each of these four chapters.

Do make early and frequent use of the Demonstration Lessons which, for convenience, are together at the end of the book. They will show you, step by step, how to play a simple piano piece, scales and *arpeggios*, and how to read music at sight. The basic principles in these lessons are of vital importance, as also are those discussed in Chapter 7 (How to Practise); this chapter should be studied at a fairly early stage. Chapter 14 (Tension and Relaxation) is also, I think, of great importance, and has been the subject of my concern for many years.

If, after reading this book, you feel that you would prefer to work to a more rigid (and less personal) plan than the one I have suggested, then one of the published methods which is divided into lessons could be studied side by side with this book. One such method is *Piano Lessons with Fanny Waterman and Marion Harewood*, Books One to Three (Faber Music).

If you are using this book to teach a young child, the books of studies and pieces cited should be replaced by one or two of the many small albums which are specially written for children. Some of these are so attractively produced and illustrated, that perhaps the best course might be to ask your dealer to produce a suitable selection, and allow the child to make the choice. The series of *Piano Books* by Carol Barratt and Wendy Hole (Chester Music), and the *Piano Albums for Children* (Universal Edition) are particularly good examples of attractive productions.

2

The Instrument

The piano action

Although the early keyboard instruments contributed something to the modern piano, their actions are quite different. The clavichord has the simplest and most direct action, housed in an oblong box; a key, when depressed by a gentle rocking motion of the fingers, causes a brass blade (called a 'tangent') to touch the string. The harpsichord, whose shape is somewhat similar to that of the modern grand piano, has an action in which the strings are plucked by plectra (of quill or leather) set at right angles in wooden 'jacks' which rise when a key is depressed and then fall back into position. Harpsichords have several sets of strings, and sometimes two or more keyboards, and hand-stops and pedals. Virginals (rectangular) and spinets (five-sided or triangular) have single keyboards with one set of strings, which are also plucked by plectra. In the sixteenth century, a small virginal was often placed on top of a larger one, thus forming a 'pair of virginals'.

The modern piano action is based on the idea of the Italian, Bartolomeo Cristofori who, about 1709, introduced a keyboard mechanism fitted with hammers (instead of harpsichord jacks), capable of producing loud and soft (*piano* and *forte*) sounds; from this we get the word 'pianoforte'.

If you look inside a grand piano, you will see that the strings are arranged in groups: the higher notes have three strings to each note, and each of the lower notes has either two thicker strings or a single thick string. If you press down a key fairly quickly you will see that a felt-covered hammer will strike the string (or group of strings) and that whether the key is held down or released the hammer will at once fall back, so that the string is free to vibrate. A felt-lined 'damper' will also spring away from the string when the key is depressed, and fall back on the string when the key is released, thus stopping the sound. The shortest strings, having very little sustaining power, are not fitted with dampers.

The quantity of sound (i.e. the loudness or softness) that can be obtained from a piano string depends upon the extent to which the string is made to vibrate, and this in turn depends upon the amount of energy with which the piano key is depressed. If put down very slowly indeed the hammer may not reach the string, and there will be no sound. If depressed a little faster there will be a soft sound and, as the speed of depression is increased, so the sound will also increase in loudness. An important characteristic of piano sound is that once a string has been struck, the sound will immediately begin to fade. The pianist, unlike most other performers (e.g. violinist, flautist) is thus unable either to maintain a single sound at a constant level, or to increase or diminish it at will.

The pedals

The modern piano usually has two pedals. The one on the right is the 'damper' or 'sustaining' pedal (often miscalled the 'loud' pedal). The effect of this pedal is to keep the dampers raised from the strings so that the notes which have been sounded will continue to sound when the keys are released until the vibrations of the strings come to an end. Since the damper pedal raises *all* the dampers, it releases, in addition to the note sounded when a key is depressed, a series of higher and weaker sounds called 'partials' or 'harmonics'. Although these partials are normally unheard, unless they are made prominent, they do help to enrich the sound. A simple experiment will illustrate this. Depress the damper pedal and hold it down, then depress Middle C key with some force (see Example 3.2 for position of Middle C). Now *silently* depress the C key next above Middle C (having found its position from Example 3.2), and release both the damper pedal and the Middle C key. The upper C (being a partial of Middle C) will continue to sound because its damper is still raised, though the other dampers have fallen. This harmonic enrichment has to be taken into account when using the damper pedal. When conflicting harmonies occur, the pianist has to decide whether or not the resultant clash is artistically desirable.

Some pianos, such as the Steinway, have a third, middle pedal. This 'sostenuto' pedal, when used instead of the damper pedal, keeps certain dampers up when it is depressed, while allowing other dampers to remain down, and thus enables the performer to sustain an isolated note or chord (mainly below Middle C), while higher changing notes are not affected.

The left pedal (called 'soft' or *una corda*) is used to reduce or alter the quality of sound. On upright pianos this pedal, when depressed, usually moves the hammers closer to the strings, so that they travel a shorter distance with less speed. On grand pianos it moves the keyboard and hammers sideways, so that two strings instead of three (or one instead of two) are struck.

The damper pedal is used frequently; the soft pedal infrequently. Either may be used on its own, or both together.

Choosing a piano

If you are buying a piano the choice needs to be made with care as a good piano is a very costly instrument. Pianos are made in many shapes and sizes. Grand pianos, in which the strings are horizontal, are usually considerably more expensive than upright pianos in similar condition; the larger grands are not suitable for small rooms, although baby grands take up very little space. Upright pianos vary in size and structure, and although the tone of the largest upright may compare favourably with that of a small grand, small upright pianos often have a much weaker tone. Most good upright pianos are over-strung, the strings being arranged diagonally, one set crossing the other; the length of the bass strings is thus greater, and the tone fuller, than that of vertically strung pianos. The dampers are usually under the hammers, but are sometimes over them; the under damper system is usually better, since it gives more weight to the keys.

If the purchase of a secondhand piano is contemplated, and it has not been reconditioned by a reputable piano repairer, it is usually essential to have the piano inspected by an expert, as the cost of restoring a neglected piano may be excessive. Some of the defects to look out for are rusty strings, warped hammers and dampers, a cracked sound-board, worn or moth-ridden felts, pedals which stick or rattle, a stiff action, and ivory keys which are nearly worn through. If faults such as these exist, only an expert can judge whether restoration is possible and worthwhile.

Apart from outright cash purchase, it is possible to buy a new piano on a five year purchase plan, or to rent a piano (credit sometimes being given for part of the rental charge, if purchase is decided upon at the end of a specified period). Local instrument dealers will usually supply details. It is also sometimes possible to arrange to use a piano at a school or church hall for regular practice – perhaps in return for a small donation.

Looking after a piano

A piano does not improve with age: if subjected to hours of practice a day, it will eventually show signs of wear and tear. Hammer and damper felts will develop ridges where they come in contact with the strings, and, unless renewed, the tone will be affected (sometimes, as a temporary measure, the hammer felts can be 'pricked'). Nevertheless, a good piano can last a century or more if it is properly looked after and regularly played.

The position of the piano is important. It should not be in a draught (e.g. under an open window), and it should never be put into a room, or against an outside wall, which is damp: if it is, rust may form on the strings, and the hammers and dampers may warp. Central heating may also cause grave problems. Although a piano should not be left for long winter periods in a room without heat (this is unlikely if it is regularly played on), a position close to a hot radiator may not only play havoc with the tuning, but may also cause the sound-board to crack. If central heating is unavoidable, the use of a suitable humidifier may be the only way to alleviate the situation.

A piano needs to be tuned at regular intervals by an experienced tuner, who is also able to deal with any other problems which may arise. Good tuners are in short supply, but it may be possible to make a contract with one of the leading piano makers or suppliers for a piano to be tuned two or three times a year. As a first step a local music shop may be able to offer advice. It is as well to ask the tuner to keep your piano up to standard *pitch* (A = 440 cycles a second).[1] If you wish to check the pitch yourself you can buy a small metal tuning fork from your music dealer.

Should anything go wrong with the piano action it is wise not to touch it yourself, but to leave it to an expert; it is quite easy to break a hammer or string.

[1] *Pitch* is used to describe how high or low a particular sound is, see page 12

3

Theory of Piano Music (1)

The pattern of the keyboard

Look at the piano keyboard, and you will see that the white and black keys form a regular pattern, with the white keys at equal distances from each other, and the black keys grouped in twos and threes.

Example 3.1

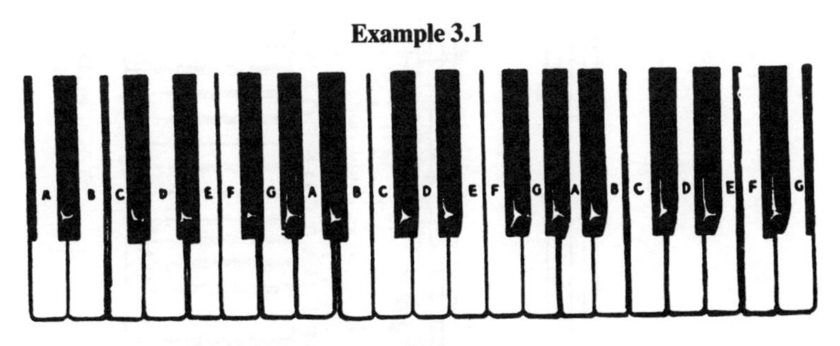

This basic pattern is repeated throughout the entire length of the keyboard. Depress, with one finger, the white keys in order, starting from the extreme left of the keyboard, and you will hear the sounds becoming gradually higher until, at the extreme right, the highest sound is reached. Look inside the piano, and you will see the shorter and thinner the string, the higher the sound or pitch.

Now look at Example 3.2, which is a diagram of the complete keyboard on the average piano (some pianos have extra keys). Please ignore, for the moment, the music notation above the keyboard diagram, this will be explained very shortly.

Example 3.2

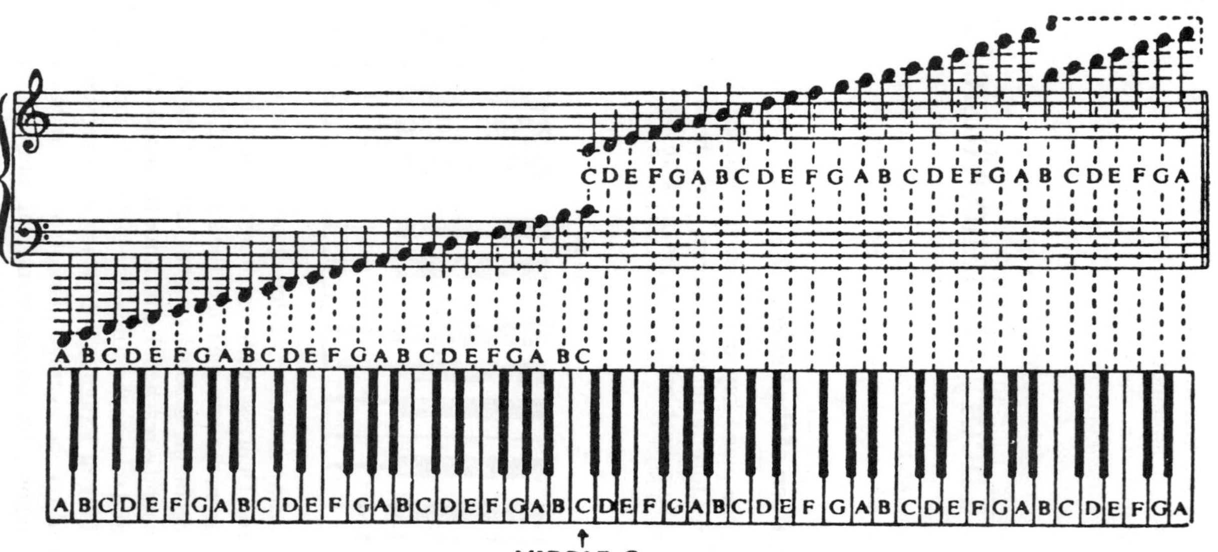

CDEFGABCDEFGABCDEFGABCDEFGA
ABCDEFGABCDEFGABCDEFGABC
ABCDEFGABCDEFGABCDEFGABCDEFGABCDEFGABCDEFGABCDEFGA
MIDDLE C

You will see that the white keys are named after the first seven letters of the alphabet – ABCDEFG – and that this series is repeated each time the seventh letter (G) is reached; also that the white keys immediately to the left and right of the *two* black keys are, respectively, C and E, and the white keys immediately to the left and right of the *three* black keys are, respectively, F and B.

Your first task is to memorise the pattern of the piano keys; to know the names of the white keys, and to be able to find them on the piano. Start by naming (and playing with one finger) all the As, Bs, Cs etc. on the keyboard. When you can do this easily, try naming different white piano keys at random, and finding them on the keyboard.

The *average* piano keyboard has fifty white keys, seven of which are C keys; of these seven keys, the fourth C from the left (or right) is known as *Middle C*. Middle C is a 'landmark', and it is important that you should memorise its position, so that you can find it quickly, as this will help you to read from printed music. Its position should be studied carefully; first from Example 3.2, and then on the piano keyboard.

How piano music is written

Piano music is written on two sets of five parallel lines called *staves*. These staves, which are bracketed together, are distinguished from one another by two different signs called *clefs*. The *treble clef* (𝄞) is normally placed on the upper stave, and the *bass clef* (𝄢) on the lower stave. The treble clef is also known as the 'G' clef, because the lower part of the clef sign encloses the note G. The bass clef is also known as the 'F' clef, because a pair of dots is placed on either side of the fourth (F) line.

Example 3.3

Musical sounds of different pitch (i.e. height or depth) are shown by little oval characters called *notes*, which are placed on the lines of the stave, and in the spaces between the lines. In addition, a note may be placed above each stave, and another note below the stave. Usually, treble notes on the upper stave are played with the right hand, and bass notes on the lower stave with the left hand.

In theory, the treble and bass staves may be combined to form a single *great stave* of eleven lines and ten spaces, with the names of the notes in alphabetical order; in practice, two five-line staves are easier to read. The middle (sixth) line of the great stave is then introduced on a short line, either below the treble stave, or above the bass stave, if a note appears on it; this note is then called Middle C (Example 3.4).

You should now memorise the names of the notes on the lines, and in the spaces, of each stave. You will find it easier to do this if the lines are separated from the spaces.

You may find it helpful to associate the names of the notes with a sentence or word, e.g.

Treble notes on the lines:	Every Good Boy Deserves Favour.
Treble notes in the spaces:	FACE
Bass notes on the lines:	Gold Buttons Dress Fine Actors.
Bass notes in the spaces:	All Cars Expect Grease.

(If you make up your own sentences, you may find them easier to remember – Example 3.5.)

Example 3.4

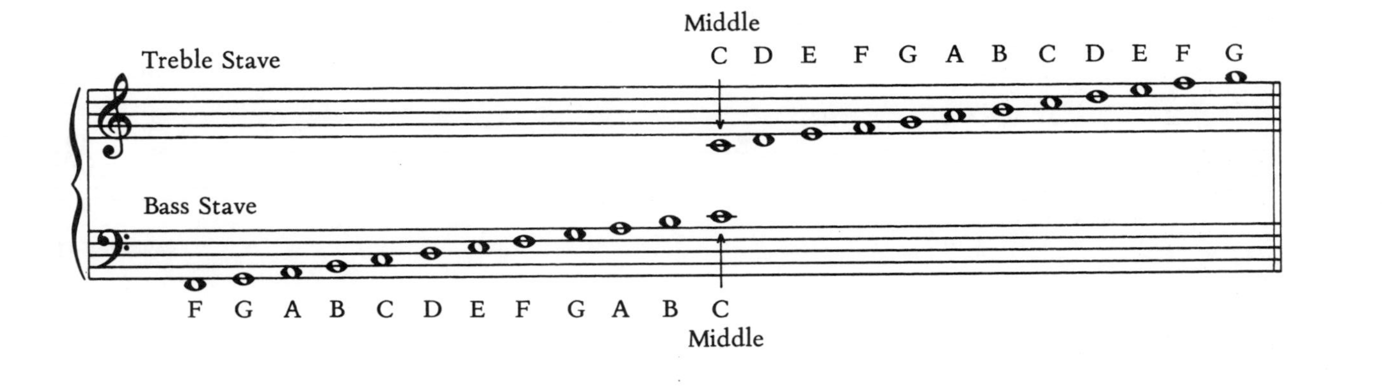
Middle
C D E F G A B C D E F G
Treble Stave
Bass Stave
F G A B C D E F G A B C
Middle

Example 3.5

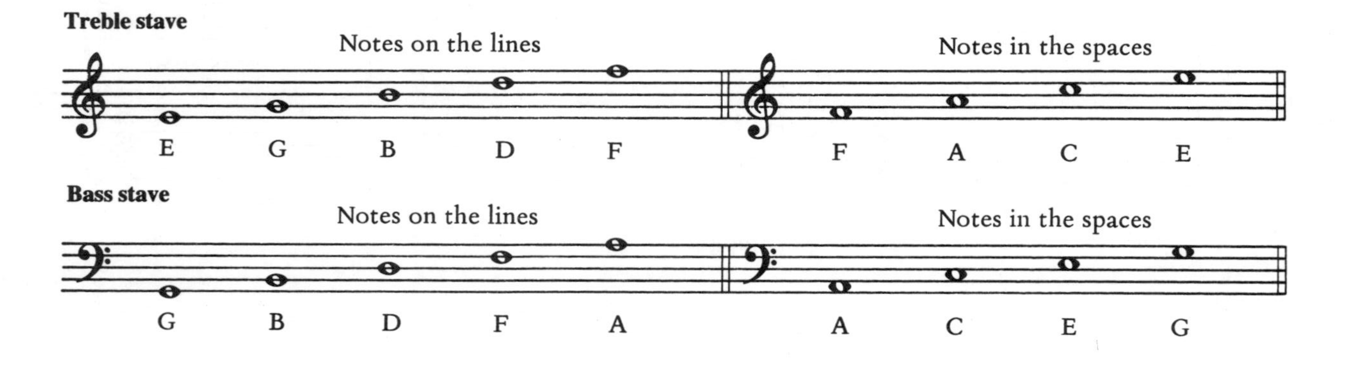
Treble stave
Notes on the lines
E G B D F
Notes in the spaces
F A C E
Bass stave
Notes on the lines
G B D F A
Notes in the spaces
A C E G

The octave

The distance from any white note to the next white note of the same name on the piano keyboard is called an *octave* (i.e. eight notes). (Although the notation of the black piano keys has not yet been discussed, it should be noted that the distance from any black note to the next black note of the same name is also an octave.) Thus, Example 3.6 (a), which is Middle C on the piano, is an octave below (b), and an octave above (c).

From the diagram of the piano keyboard (Example 3.2) you will see that the *average* piano has seven octaves, starting and finishing on the note A.

Example 3.6

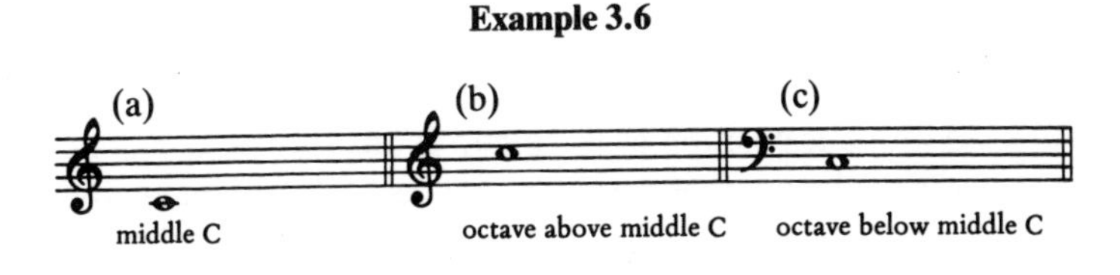

Self-testing questions

Preliminary remarks

Write the answers to these questions in your music book, without reference to this chapter. Check each answer with the appropriate music example (the number of this is shown in brackets at the end of the question). In a few questions, a page of the text is given, instead of, or as well as, the number of the music example. If your answer is wrong, try the question again.

1 Write, on a stave in your music book, a treble clef sign. Then write: a) the five notes on the lines; b) the four notes in the spaces. Put a letter name under each note. (*Example 3.5*)
2 Do the same with the bass clef. (*Example 3.5*)
3 Write on the stave: (a) Middle C in the treble clef; (b) Middle C in the bass clef. (*Example 3.4*)
4 Write these notes in the treble clef: (a) A in a space; (b) D on a line; (c) E in a space; (d) E on a line. (*Example 3.5*)
5 Write these notes in the bass clef: (a) G in a space; (b) D on a line; (c) G on a line; (d) A in a space. (*Example 3.5*)
6 Write: (a) the C above Middle C in the treble clef; (b) the C below Middle C in the bass clef. (*Example 3.6*)

4

Beginning to Play

Your position at the piano

Advice about your position at the piano is only possible in general terms as much depends on variable factors such as height, build, length of arms, legs and fingers. So that while it can be said that you should sit at the centre of the keyboard, your distance from it, and the height of your seat, are to some extent matters of individual choice. If you have an adjustable piano stool you will be able, by experiment, to find the height that suits you best. If you use a chair, adjust the height, if necessary, by adding a cushion, and be careful to sit well forward. There is no 'correct' height; some pianists prefer a fairly high seat, others a fairly low one.

In general, you should sit at such a height, and at such a distance from the keyboard, that when your arms are naturally bent, your fingers will fall easily on the white keys, and just about reach the black keys when your fingers are stretched out a little.

This means, for example, that if the thumb is playing a white key, it will normally be in the same position whether the next key to be played is white or black; if the thumb is playing a black key, however, it will be stretched forward, and the whole hand positioned over the black keys.

Your elbows should hang loosely and naturally, fairly close to the body, and not be lifted too high. As a rough guide, your forearms need to be almost level with the keyboard, and your elbows a little higher. The ball of your right foot (not the toe) should rest firmly on the damper (right hand) pedal, ready for action. As the left pedal is used less frequently, the left leg can be further back (perhaps just in front of the piano stool). At times the left leg can carry the weight of the body, so it is worth experimenting to find a position which seems natural and comfortable.

Your hands should normally be cup-shaped (imagine you are holding an orange in each hand), so that the fingers are bent and rounded, with the tips playing vertically into the centre of the keys; your finger nails will need to be kept short. The thumb plays with the side, not the tip, and should be slightly bent so that it rests on the key about as far as the root of the nail. These finger positions are only approximate, and modifications may be necessary when black keys and certain styles of playing are involved.

How fingering is indicated

In modern piano music, notes to be played by the thumb of either hand are numbered 1, and notes to be played by the other fingers, in order, 2,3,4,5. These small figures are printed above or below certain notes. Some music (usually advanced) is not fingered at all, and the pianist has to work out suitable fingering in accordance with general principles which will be discussed later in this book. (Should you come across music which was printed in England many years ago, an obsolete form of fingering may be used, in which the thumb is marked with a +, and the fingers, in order, 1,2,3,4.)

Finding notes on the piano

The preliminary exercises in Example 4.1 will help you to read printed music and to find notes on the piano. You should first name the notes in each group, and then play them. At first you may do this by looking down at the keyboard, finding the first note of each group, and then playing all the notes without looking at the music. As soon as possible, however, you should practise these exercises without looking at your hands.

Be careful to use the fingering printed below each exercise. You will see that where notes proceed in alphabetical order, the fingers are used in that order, but that if a white key is left out, the corresponding finger is also left out. This is more fully explained in

Example 4.1

1 (a) C D E F G F E D C (b) G A B C D C B A G (c) C D E F G F E D C

1 2 3 4 5 4 3 2 1 1 2 3 4 5 4 3 2 1 1 2 3 4 5 4 3 2 1

2 (a) G A B C D C B A G (b) C D E F G F E D C (c) G A B C B A G

5 4 3 2 1 2 3 4 5 5 4 3 2 1 2 3 4 5 5 4 3 2 3 4 5

3 (a) C E G (b) D B G (c) C A F (d) C E G

1 3 4 5 3 1 5 3 1 1 3 5

4 (a) G B D (b) G E C (c) A F D (d) F A C

5 3 1 1 3 5 1 3 5 5 3 1

Example 4.2

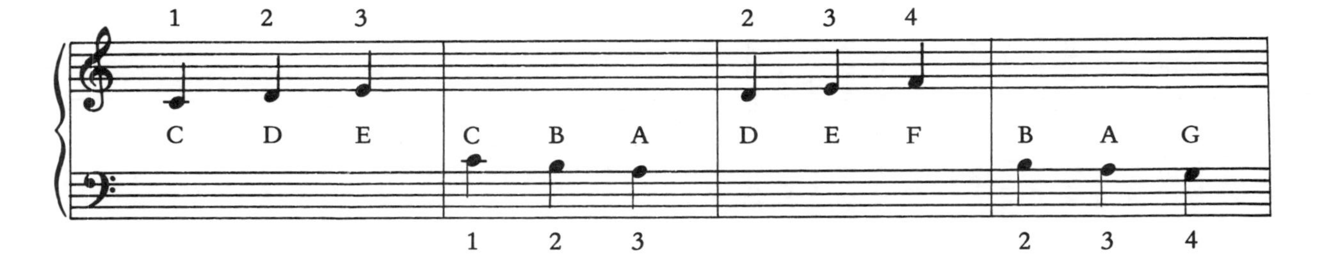

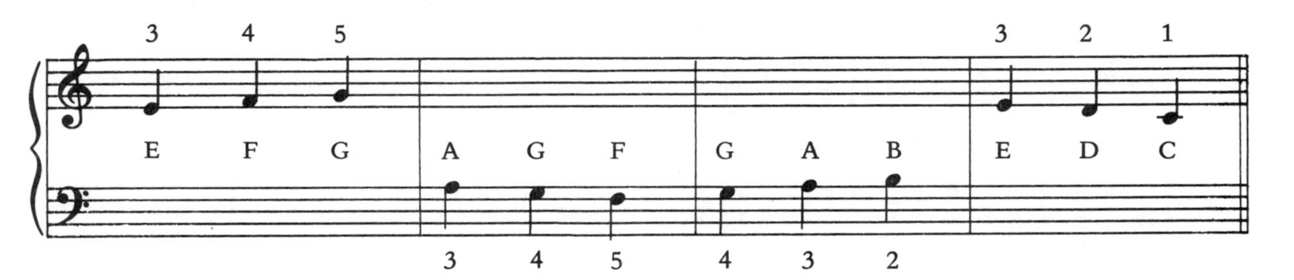

Chapter 8. To help you, the names of the notes are printed above each exercise. Exercise 1(a), starts on Middle C; if you are uncertain where to find this, or the other starting notes, on the piano, please refer to the diagram of the keyboard in Example 3.2.

You can now play the short exercise in Example 4.2, using the fingering which is marked. The first three notes are played with the right hand, and the next three notes with the left; both hands start on Middle C. In this exercise, every note is of equal value. Play fairly softly and as smoothly as you can. Try to raise one key at the precise moment that you depress the next, so that there are no gaps between sounds.

You could also start one of the books of easy studies (see page 2). At this stage, it is quite in order, if you wish, to write the names of the notes in pencil, so that you can rub them out as soon as you feel confident enough to read them without this aid. Also, since it is quite easy to play in the wrong octave, it is wise to check, from Example 3.2, the relative position of the written note with the note on the keyboard.

5

Theory of Piano Music (2)

Leger lines

If we add together the number of notes which can be written on the lines, and in the spaces, of the two staves, and also include the single notes above and below the staves, together with Middle C, we have a total of twenty-three notes. But since there are fifty white notes on the average piano, short *leger lines*[1] are used when notes are too high, or too low, to be written on the staves (the little line on which Middle C is written is, in fact, a leger line).

The names of the notes on the leger lines above and below the treble and bass staves are shown in Example 5.1.

Example 5.1

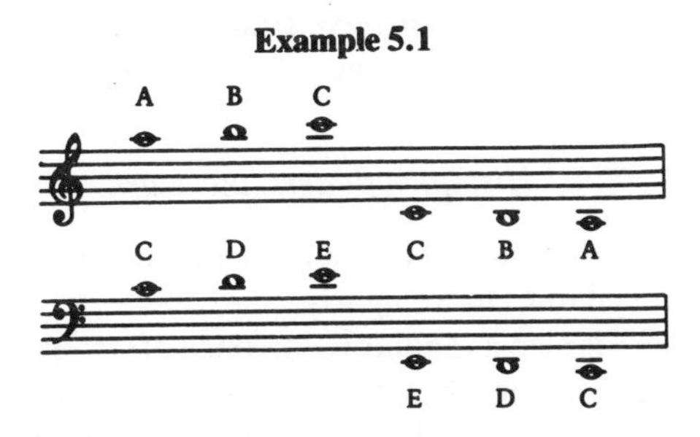

You can, if you wish, memorise these notes, but you may find it easier to learn them gradually, as they occur in the music you are playing.

[1] Only a few leger lines will be found in easy piano music. Additional lines, which occur in more difficult music, are shown in Example 3.2.

Octave signs

Since high leger lines are often difficult to read, the sign *8va* (or 8) may be placed above certain notes, which are then played an octave higher than they are written. When the sign *8va* or *8va bassa* is placed *below* notes, these are to be played an octave lower.

Example 5.2

When the figure *8*, or the words *Con 8va*, are placed below a note, the written note and the note an octave below it must be played together.

Beats and bars

At some time or other you may have scanned poetry to determine its structure, and the number of 'feet' in a line. If, for instance, you were scanning:

His Spírit flútters líke a lárk

you might stress those syllables marked with an accent(´), and pass over the other syllables more lightly.

In music there is also a regular recurrence of stronger and weaker accents, or *beats*. Strong beats can be separated by one or more weaker beats and beats can be grouped into rhythmic[1] units called

[1] Rhythm, though hard to define, takes in everything connected with the 'time' side of music (beats, bars, accents, phrases, etc.). But it goes much deeper than this, implying natural, living, 'breathing' performance, as opposed to mere mechanical time-keeping and accuracy. It might be called the 'heart beat' of music.

bars, which are marked by drawing perpendicular lines across the stave, called *bar-lines*.

Example 5.3

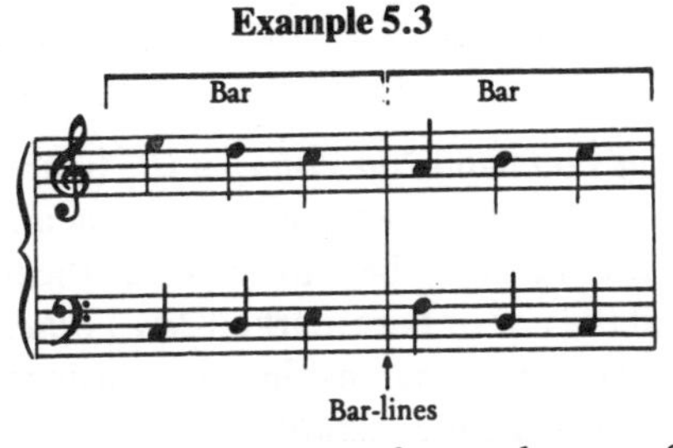

Each bar may consist of a group of two, three or four beats, and the beat immediately after each bar-line is normally the most strongly accented.

Example 5.4

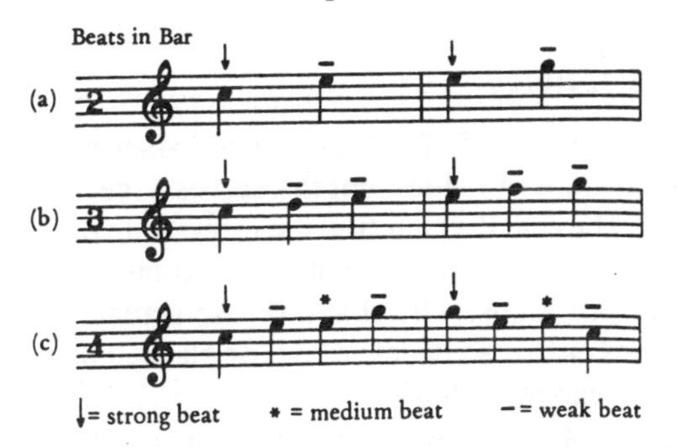

You will see that in Example 5.4 the bars of two and three beats consist of a strong beat followed by one or two weaker beats; but that in the bar of four beats the first beat receives the strong accent, the third beat a medium accent, and the second and fourth beats weaker accents.

Double-bars, repeat marks and signs

Two bar-lines placed together are called a *double-bar*, and are used to mark the end of a movement. Dots placed to the left of a double-bar mean that the preceding movement is to be repeated. Placed to the right of a double-bar they mean that the movement which follows is to be repeated (Example 5.5).

Example 5.5

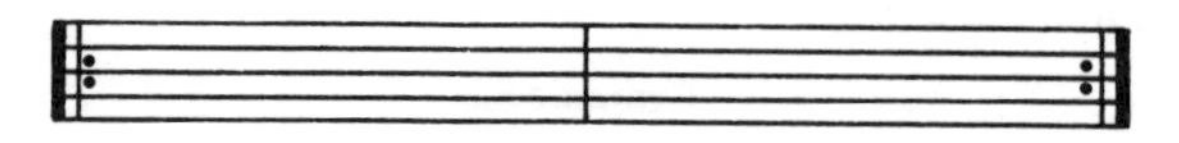

The words *1ma Volta* and *2da Volta*, or the figures *1* and *2*, when printed over bars where a repetition occurs, mean that the bar or bars marked *1ma Volta* are to be omitted when the music is played a second time, and the bar or bars marked *2da Volta* played instead.

The sign *DC (Da Capo)* means that the music is to be repeated from the beginning of the movement.

The sign *DS (Dal Segno)* means that the music is to be repeated from the sign 𝄋.

The word *Fine* (the end) is sometimes placed over a double-bar to mark the conclusion of the piece.

The values of notes

If all melodies consisted of notes of equal value, music would be a dull affair (Example 4.2 does, but this serves a special purpose, and could scarcely be called a beautiful melody). So in order to show the length of time that different sounds are to last, we use notes of several different kinds. The shape of the actual notehead is the same, but the centre can be left white, or blacked in,[1] and different kinds of 'tails' can be added.

Example 5.6 shows the appearance of each kind of note, and its value in relation to other kinds of notes. The English names are used in this book, although the American names are perhaps more logical, since they show at a glance the relative values of different notes, by dividing whole notes into fractions.

When writing music, the tail of a note is usually upwards if the head is below the third line of the stave and downwards if the head is above the third line. If the head is *on* the third line, the tail can go either way. With chords, or part-writing, this may not apply. It is as well to study some printed piano music, to exemplify this.

[1] Several times in my teaching career I have been asked whether this has any connection with the white and black keys of the piano, so perhaps I had better say that it has not.

Example 5.6

English term
American term
Semibreve
Whole Note
is equal to
2 Minims
Half Notes
or
4 Crotchets
Quarter Notes;
or
8 Quavers
8th Notes
or
16 Semiquavers
16th Notes
or
32 Demisemiquavers
32nd Notes

Dotted notes

A dot placed after a note increases its value by one half. A dotted semibreve is therefore equal to an undotted semibreve plus a minim. The effect of placing dots after each kind of note is shown in Example 5.7.

Example 5.7

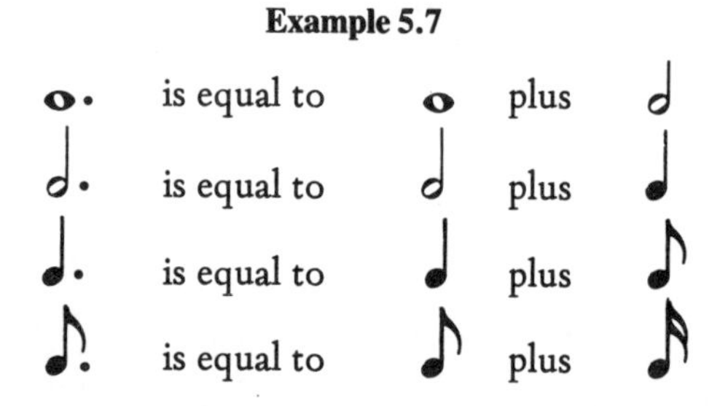

(Two dots (less usual) increase the value of a note by three-quarters.)

Time-signatures

Figures called *time-signatures* appear at the beginning of a piece of music, immediately after the clef signs on the stave. They may also appear during the course of a movement, if the original time-signature is changed.

Example 5.8

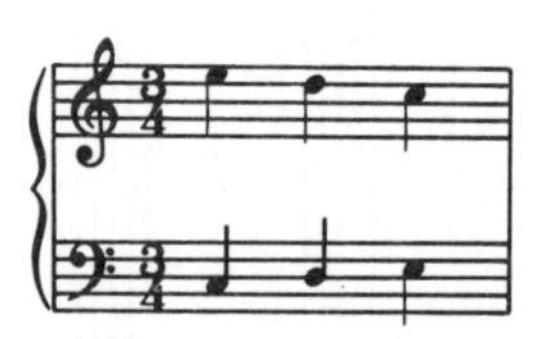

The upper figure shows the number of beats in each bar; the lower figure the value of each beat. Thus the time-signature in Example 5.8 shows that there are three beats, each of the value of a crotchet, in a bar.

The notes which make up a bar of music will not necessarily be of the same duration as the beats. A bar of $\frac{4}{4}$ time, for example, might contain four crotchets, or might consist of any combination of notes which are the equivalent of four crotchets.

In Example 5.9, bar one contains one semibreve; bar two, two minims; bar three, eight quavers; and bar four, one minim, one crotchet and two quavers; but each bar contains the equivalent of four crotchets.

Example 5.9

Similarly, a bar of $\frac{2}{4}$ time contains two crotchets or their equivalents, and a bar of $\frac{3}{4}$ time three crotchets or their equivalents.

Each beat in a bar may have the value of a plain (i.e. undotted) note. This is called *simple time*, and each beat may be divided into halves, quarters, etc. Alternatively, each beat may have the value of a dotted note; this is called *compound time*, and each beat may be divided into thirds, sixths, etc. Example 5.10 will make this clearer.

Example 5.10

Baa, Baa, Black Sheep

Example 5.11 shows the time-signatures in common use, together with the value in notes of one complete bar. Bars which may be divided into two, three or four equal beats are said to be, respectively, in *duple, triple* and *quadruple* time. (Note that the alternative signs, 𝄵 for $\frac{2}{2}$ for **C** for $\frac{4}{4}$, are sometimes found in early editions of music. They are now less often used, as past inconsistencies tended to make them confusing.)

Example 5.11

	SIMPLE TIMES		COMPOUND TIMES	
	Time Signature	Value of one bar	Time Signature	Value of one bar
DUPLE	¢ or 2/2	𝅗𝅥 𝅗𝅥	6/4	𝅗𝅥. 𝅗𝅥.
	2/4	♩ ♩	6/8	♩. ♩.
	2/8	♪ ♪	6/16	♪. ♪.
TRIPLE	3/2	𝅗𝅥 𝅗𝅥 𝅗𝅥	9/4	𝅗𝅥. 𝅗𝅥. 𝅗𝅥.
	3/4	♩ ♩ ♩	9/8	♩. ♩. ♩.
	3/8	♪ ♪ ♪	9/16	♪. ♪. ♪.
QUADRUPLE	4/2	𝅗𝅥 𝅗𝅥 𝅗𝅥 𝅗𝅥	12/4	𝅗𝅥. 𝅗𝅥. 𝅗𝅥. 𝅗𝅥.
	C or 4/4	♩ ♩ ♩ ♩	12/8	♩. ♩. ♩. ♩.
	4/8	♪ ♪ ♪ ♪	12/16	♪. ♪. ♪. ♪.

Grouping of notes

In printed music, notes are often grouped together by joining the hooks of their tails.

Example 5.12

In simple time, notes, when joined, are grouped in twos, fours, eights, etc. In compound time they are grouped in threes, sixes, nines, twelves, etc.

Example 5.13

Simple times

Compound times

Occasionally, three notes may be played in the time of two notes of similar value. The group of three notes is then called a *triplet*, and the sign $\widehat{3}$ is placed above it.

Example 5.14

Other irregular groupings are sometimes used:

Name	*Sign*	*Effect*
Duplet	$\widehat{2}$	Two notes played in the time of three.
Quadruplet	$\widehat{4}$	Four notes played in the time of three.
Quintuplet	$\widehat{5}$	Five notes played in the time of four.
Sextolet	$\widehat{6}$	Six notes played in the time of four.
Septuplet	$\widehat{7}$	Seven notes played in the time of four (or, occasionally, six)

Rests

In music there are often short periods of silence between sounds, and to represent them a set of signs called *rests* is used. Each rest is equivalent in duration to a note of the same value.

Some rests are rather similar, and may be confused. The semibreve rest *hangs* from the fourth line of the stave, whereas the minim rest *sits* on the third line. Also, when the sign ꞁ̊ is used to represent the crotchet rest, the hook is to the right; the sign for the quaver rest is similar, but the hook is to the left (see example 5.15).

A silent bar is indicated by a semibreve rest; several bars' silence is shown by a rest with a number over it.

A pause 𝄐 over a note or rest means that it is to be prolonged a little; the exact length is left to the performer's discretion.

Example 5.15

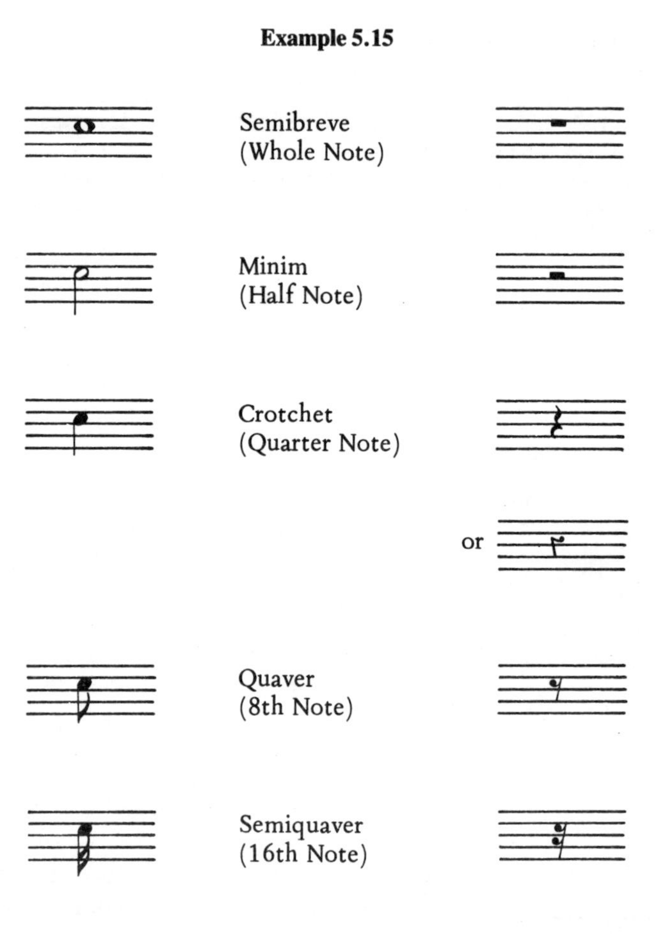
Semibreve
(Whole Note)
Minim
(Half Note)
Crotchet
(Quarter Note)
or
Quaver
(8th Note)
Semiquaver
(16th Note)
Demisemiquaver
(32nd Note)

Self-testing questions

(Please see preliminary remarks in Chapter 3, page 15.)

1 (a) Write the notes C, D, E, F on the treble stave, and write above them the sign which indicates that these notes are to be played an octave *higher* than they are written. (b) Write the notes F, E, D, C on the bass stave, and write below them the sign(s) which indicate that these notes are to be played an octave *lower* than written. (*Example 5.2*)

2 Write notes on the first three leger lines (a) above the treble stave; (b) below the treble stave; (c) above the bass stave; (d) below the bass stave. (*Example 5.1*)

3 'Beats' are grouped into rhythmic units. What are these called, and how are they 'marked'? (*Example 5.3*)

4 (a) Which beat in a bar is normally the most strongly accented? (b) In a bar of two or three beats, which are the 'weak' beats? (c) In a bar of four beats, which is the 'medium' beat, and which are the 'weak' beats? (*Example 5.4*)

5 What is a 'double-bar', and how is it shown on the stave? (*Example 5.5*)

6 Write on the stave, a note which has the value of (a) a semibreve, or whole note; (b) a minim, or half note; (c) a crotchet, or quarter note; (d) a quaver, or 8th note; (e) a semiquaver, or 16th note; (f) a demisemiquaver, or 32nd note. (*Example 5.6*)

7 (a) What is the effect of a dot placed after a note? (b) What is the equivalent of a dotted semibreve? (*Example 5.7*)

8 Write, on the stave, the time-signature of $\frac{3}{4}$. What do each of these figures mean? (*Example 5.8*)

9 Write three bars in $\frac{4}{4}$ time, containing the following notes: Bar one: one semibreve; Bar two: two minims; Bar three: eight quavers. (*Example 5.9*)

10 What is the difference between simple and compound times? Write (a) a bar of crotchets in $\frac{2}{4}$ time; (b) a bar of quavers in $\frac{6}{8}$ time. (*Example 5.10*)

11 Write notes to the value in beats of one bar, of each of the following times (e.g. one bar in $\frac{4}{4}$ time = ♩♩♩♩): (a) $\frac{2}{2}$; (b) $\frac{6}{4}$; (c) $\frac{3}{4}$; (d) $\frac{4}{2}$; (e) $\frac{9}{8}$; (f) $\frac{2}{4}$; (g) $\frac{12}{16}$. (*Example 5.11*)

12 Show how notes may be joined together by writing (a) a group of two quavers; (b) a group of four semiquavers; (c) a group of six semiquavers. (*Example 5.13*)

13 Write a 'triplet' consisting of three quavers. These three notes are played in the time of how many notes of similar value? (*Example 5.14*)

14 Write on the stave a 'rest' which is equivalent to each of the following notes: (a) semibreve; (b) minim; (c) crotchet (write two alternative rests); quaver; semiquaver; demisemiquaver. (*Example 5.15*)

15 How are the following indicated: (a) a silent bar; (b) a pause? (*See page 29*)

6

Theory of Piano Music (3)

Tones and semitones

The height or depth of a musical sound is called its *pitch*, and the difference in pitch between two sounds is called an *interval*. On the piano keyboard, some adjacent white keys have a black key in between, and some have not. Adjacent white keys which are not separated by a black key are said to be a *semitone* (or half-tone) apart; this is the smallest interval in modern music. Adjacent white keys which have a black key in between are said to be a *tone* (or whole-tone) apart.

Scales

A *scale* may be thought of as a 'ladder' of notes, but although we may ascend or descend the notes of the scale one by one, the sounds will not be the same distance apart.[1] In medieval times, church music was based on a complicated system of *modal scales*, each bearing a name borrowed from the ancient Greek word 'modes' (mode = manner). Each scale consisted of 'natural' notes with the basic range of seven notes plus the octave, which, on the piano, would be played only on the white keys. Two of these seven-note modal scales have survived in modern music. They are sometimes called *diatonic* scales (from the Greek word for 'through the tones'),

[1] Except for the *chromatic scale*, considered later in this chapter, which consists entirely of semitones.

and are of two kinds, *major* and *minor*.[1] If, starting on Middle C, you play each white piano key in order, up to the C above (or down to the C below), you will have played the scale of C *major*, one octave ascending or descending.

Degrees of the scale

In theory each note of the scale is called a *degree* and is given a name, though it is often more convenient to refer to degrees by numbers, as in Example 6.1. (Usually Roman numerals are used.)

Example 6.1

The names of the degrees, which are always counted upwards, are:

Degree	*Name*
I	*tonic,* or *key-note*
II	*supertonic*
III	*mediant*
IV	*subdominant*
V	*dominant*
VI	*submediant*
VII	*leading note*
VIII	*tonic,* or *key-note*

The eighth degree is, of course, a repetition of the tonic, or key-note, an octave higher in pitch.

The dominant, as its name implies, is the 'ruling' note of the scale. Next in importance is the tonic (which is the 'governing' note of the scale). Third in importance is the fourth degree, the subdominant. The seventh degree is called the leading note because of its strong tendency to lead to the tonic.

[1] The major scale is based on the 'Ionian Mode'; the minor scale on the 'Aeolian Mode'.

Sharps, flats and naturals

Since the scale of C major is formed entirely of natural notes, represented by the white keys of the piano, and these notes are named after the first seven letters of the alphabet (the only letters used in musical notation), how are the black piano keys represented? The answer is that a black key takes its name from the white key either immediately above or below it. Thus the white keys C and D are a tone apart, and the black key in between them may be looked upon as a semitone above C, or as a semitone below D.

If a sharp sign (♯) is placed before a natural note, it raises the pitch by a semitone; a flat sign (♭) before a natural note lowers the pitch by a semitone. Thus, a sharp before C natural makes it C sharp, and a flat before D natural makes it D flat.

Example 6.2

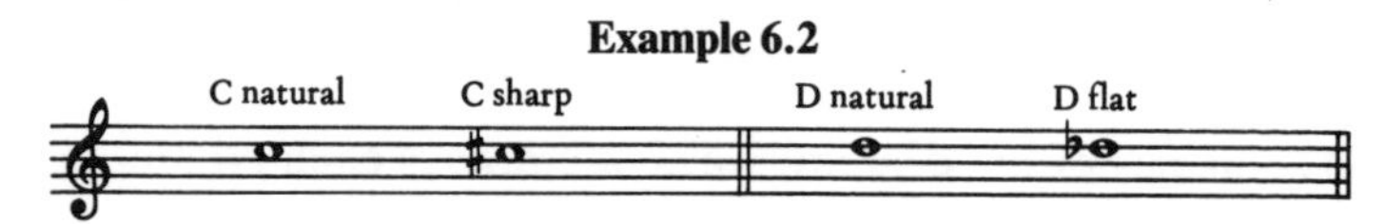

It follows, therefore, that the black piano key between the white keys C and D may be called either C sharp or D flat; and the black key between D and E may be called either D sharp or E flat, and so on. Two sounds of the same pitch, which have different letter names, are said to be *enharmonic*. Example 6.3 shows a section of the piano keyboard, with the enharmonic notes. On the piano, it is wrong to think of sharpened or flattened notes as being played only on the black keys, for example, the notes B and E, when sharpened, and C and F, when flattened, are played on white keys.

Example 6.3

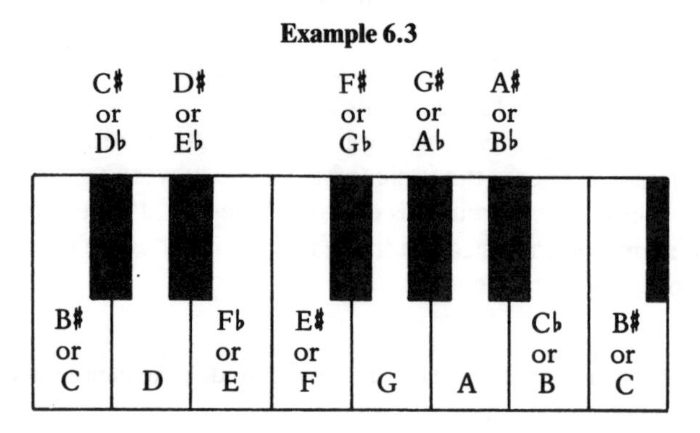

When a sharp or flat has been placed before a natural note, the original pitch can be restored to a subsequent note, of the same letter name, by placing a *natural* sign (♮) before it.

Example 6.4

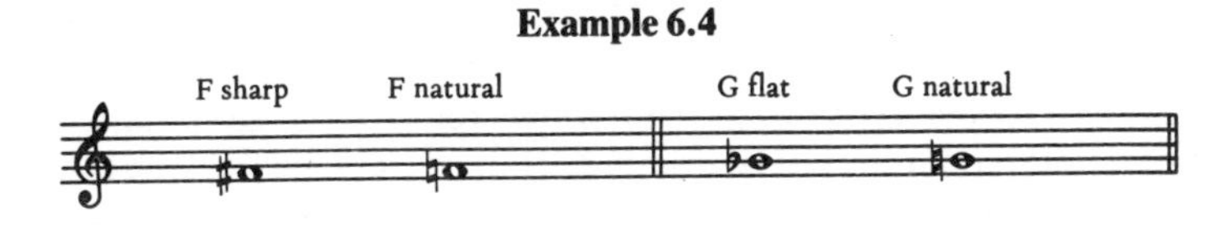

Accidentals

Accidentals are sharps and flats which are used during the course of a movement.[1] An accidental affects only the note before which it is placed, and any succeeding notes on the same line (or in the same space) on the stave, and in the *same* bar.

Example 6.5

In Example 6.5, each of the four Gs in the first bar is played as G sharp, but the G in the second bar is played as G natural. In practice, a 'cautionary' natural sign would usually be placed before this G – sometimes enclosed in a bracket (♮) – but this is not obligatory.

If a note marked with an accidental is followed by a note of the same letter name in the *same* bar, the second note may be restored to its original pitch by means of a natural sign.

Example 6.6

[1] Double-sharps and double-flats are also accidentals. These are explained on p. 45. A natural sign may also be used as an accidental. (See p. 39.)

The pattern of major scales (and key-signatures)

Looking again at the C major scale (example 6.7) you will see that the third and fourth, and the seventh and eighth notes of the scale are a semitone apart, whereas the distance between any other two adjacent notes is a tone. The eight-note scale may, in fact, be divided into two halves, each of which follows the same pattern (tone–tone–semitone). Each half is called a *tetrachord* (a Greek word applied to the four notes of an early instrument), and the two tetrachords are joined together by a tone.

Example 6.7

Scale of C Major

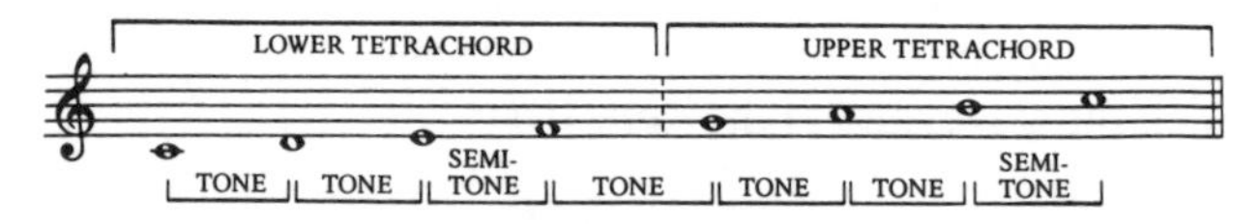

Now play, with one finger, the notes of the C major scale, carefully observing the pattern of tones and semitones on the keyboard, then write the scale in your music book.

So long as this pattern is preserved, a major scale can be formed on any tonic, or key-note. The formation of scales is, however, much easier to understand if they are studied in the right order. If we take the *upper* tetrachord of the C major scale, and add another tetrachord *above* it, we can form the scale of G major. But to preserve the pattern of each tetrachord (tone–tone–semitone) we must raise the seventh note of the new scale by a semitone. This we do by placing a sharp before the note F.

Example 6.8

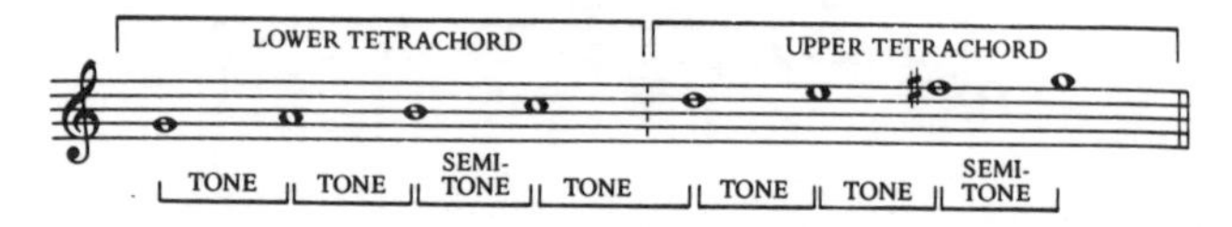

Since this sharp is a vital part of the new scale, it is placed at the beginning of the stave, immediately after the clef sign, and is called the *key-signature*. A piece of music which is founded on the G major scale is said to be in the *key* of G major.

Example 6.9

Scale of G Major

The sharp in the key-signature means that every F in the piece must be played as F sharp, unless the sharp is cancelled by a natural sign. There is thus no need to place a sharp sign before each individual F. (Now play the notes of the G major scale, and write them in your music book.)

In forming the 'sharp' series of major scales, the order goes up in fifths, so that the dominant of one key becomes the tonic of the next. To continue, therefore, we take the upper tetrachord of the G major scale, and add another tetrachord above it, thus forming the scale of D major. Again the seventh note (C) of the new scale is raised by a semitone by the addition of a sharp, so that the new key-signature has two sharps.

Example 6.10

Scale of D Major

(Now play the notes of the D major scale, and write them in your music book.)

By a similar process, we may form the major scales of A, E, B, F sharp and C sharp (key-signatures are shown in Example 6.15). You should now study the structure of these scales in your scale book, and write them in your music book.

If, instead of taking the upper tetrachord of the C major scale, we take the *lower* tetrachord and add another tetrachord *below* it, we can form the scale of F major. But to preserve the pattern of the major scale it is necessary to lower, by a semitone, the fourth note of the new scale. Thus the note B becomes B flat, and we place this flat immediately after the clef sign. It now becomes the key-signature, and affects every B that occurs in the piece. Note that, in the 'flat' series of major scales, the order goes *down* in fifths, so that the tonic of one key becomes the dominant of the next.

Example 6.11

Scale of F Major

By a similar process we can form the major scales of B flat, E flat, A flat, D flat, G flat and C flat (key-signatures shown in Example 6.15, p. 41). Again, you should study the structure of these scales in your scale book, and write them in your music book. You can now, if you wish, start to practise the C major scale, with the help of Demonstration Lesson Two, p. 133. When you can play this fluently, you can practise other scales on the lines suggested in this lesson.

The minor scale

Let us now consider the second kind of diatonic scale: the *minor scale*. A composer chooses the kind of scale which best suits the 'character' of the music. Broadly speaking, music based on the minor scale is often more expressive and less brilliant than music in major keys. Thus, one would expect a funeral march to be in a minor key, and a wedding march in a major key. But there is, of course, much sad and expressive music in major keys, and vice versa.

Although the major scale has remained unaltered during the past few centuries, the minor scale has undergone several changes. The earliest form is based on the modal scale starting on A. (You can hear what it sounds like by starting on the white piano key A, and playing eight consecutive white keys.)

Example 6.12

Modal Scale of A Minor

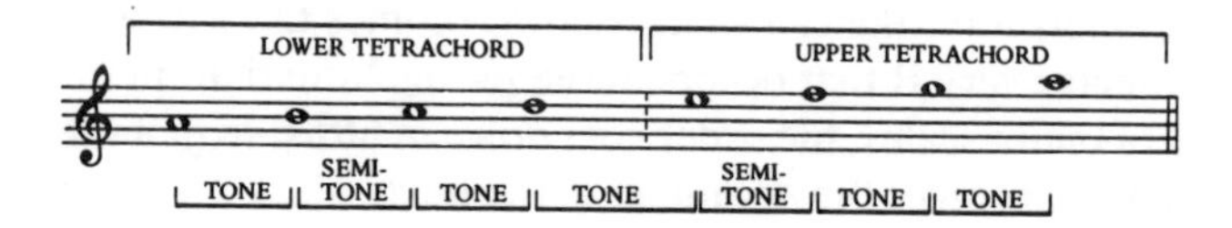

Note that, unlike the major scale, the pattern of the lower and upper tetrachords is not the same; the lower tetrachord has tone–tone–semitone; the upper tetrachord semitone–tone–tone. A peculiarity of this modal scale is that there is an interval of a tone between the seventh and eighth degrees, whereas in our modern scale system these notes are usually a semitone apart. The seventh degree is therefore usually modified. One way of doing this is to sharpen the seventh note of the modal scale. This produces what is known as the *harmonic minor* scale. Again the pattern of the two tetrachords is different.

Example 6.13

Scale of A Minor – Harmonic Form

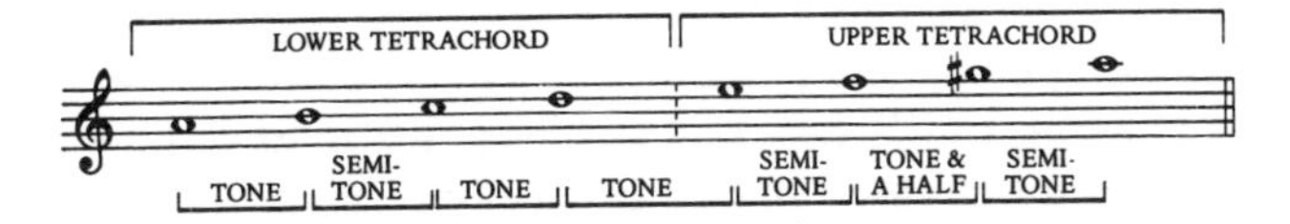

(Now play the notes of the A minor harmonic scale, and write them in your music book.)

Although the seventh note of the harmonic minor scale is sharpened, the sharp is *not* included in the key-signature, but is regarded as an accidental. (Note that sometimes a natural sign may become an 'accidental'. In the key of G major, for example, the F sharp in the key-signature, which affects every F in the piece, may be lowered a semitone by the addition of a natural sign; a subsequent note of the same letter name can be restored to its original pitch by placing a sharp before it.) However, by sharpening the seventh note, the interval between the sixth and seventh degrees of the scale becomes a tone-and-a-half (i.e. three semitones). To overcome objection to this interval (which, in vocal music, was considered difficult to sing), the *melodic minor* scale was evolved. This scale, as its name implies, was originally used chiefly for the construction of melodies, whereas the harmonic minor scale was used principally in the construction of chords (i.e. harmony).

A peculiarity of the melodic minor scale is that different forms are used when ascending and descending. In ascending, the sixth and seventh notes are sharpened; in descending, they are restored to their original pitch. Again, these sharpened notes are not included in the key-signature, but are regarded as accidentals.

Example 6.14

Scale of A Minor – Melodic Form

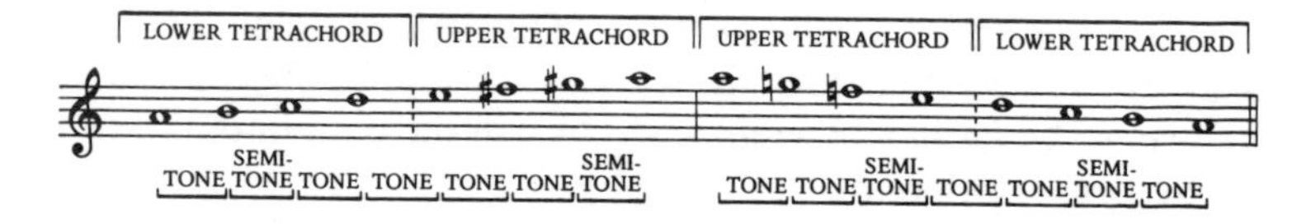

In ascending, the semitones fall between the second and third, and seventh and eighth notes; in descending they fall between the sixth and fifth, and third and second notes. The descending form is, in fact, the same as that of the modal scale. (Now play the notes of the A minor melodic scale, and write them in your music book.)

A minor scale which starts on the same note (or 'tonic') as a major scale is known as its *tonic minor*. But a glance at Example 6.15 will show that the key-signatures of a major scale and of a tonic minor scale are not the same, even though both scales start on the same note. For instance, A minor has a key-signature of no sharps or flats, whereas A major has a key-signature of three sharps.

Major and minor scales which *do* have the same key-signature, however, are said to be *relative* to one another: C major and A minor, for example, are relative because each has a key-signature of no sharps or flats. Each major scale has its *relative minor*, the first note of the minor scale being the sixth note of the relative major. Looking at it another way, the last three notes of the major scale become the first three notes of its relative minor. Example 6.15 shows the key-signatures of relative major and minor scales. As we have already seen, however, the key-signature of the harmonic and melodic scale does not fit exactly, and certain modifications are necessary.

We can now construct a series of minor scales. The process is, in some respects, similar to that of forming major scales. If we take the *upper* tetrachord of the modal scale of A minor (Example 6.12), and add another tetrachord *above* it, we can form the modal scale of E minor. But since the two tetrachords of a minor scale are not identical, we must preserve the pattern of the new lower tetrachord

Example 6.15

Key-signatures of Major and Relative Minor Scales

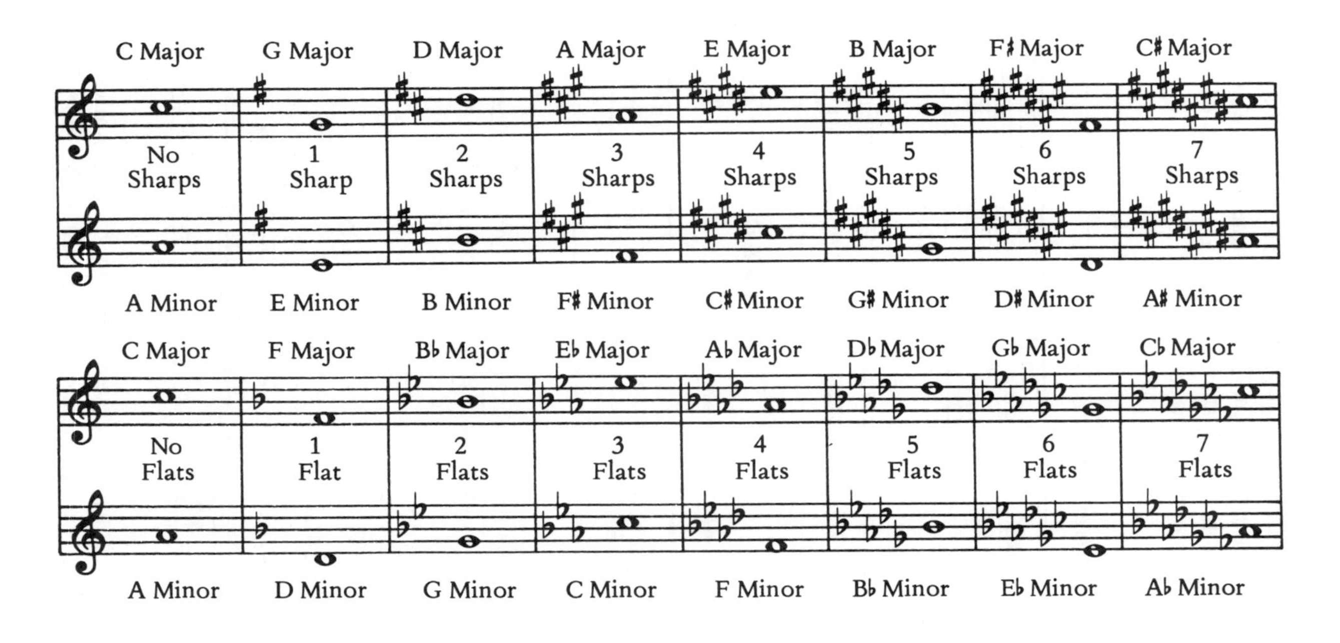

(tone–semitone–tone) by modifying the pattern of the old (formerly upper) tetrachord (semitone–tone–tone). This we do by adding a key-signature of one sharp, which has the effect of sharpening the second note of the new scale.

Example 6.16

Modal Scale of E Minor

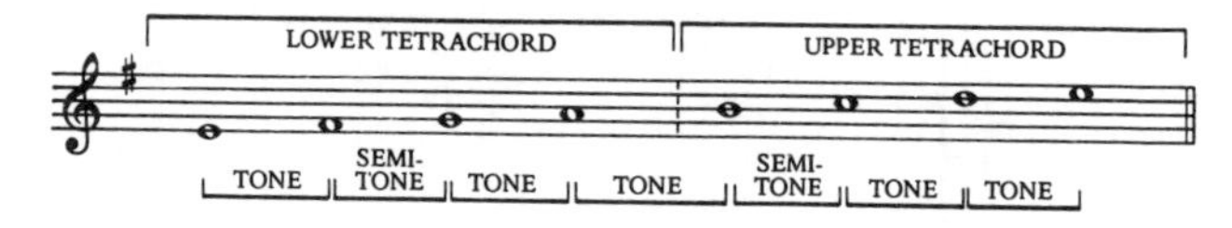

From the modal scale of E minor, we can form the harmonic scale of E minor, by sharpening the seventh note of the scale by means of an accidental.

Example 6.17

Scale of E Minor – Harmonic Form

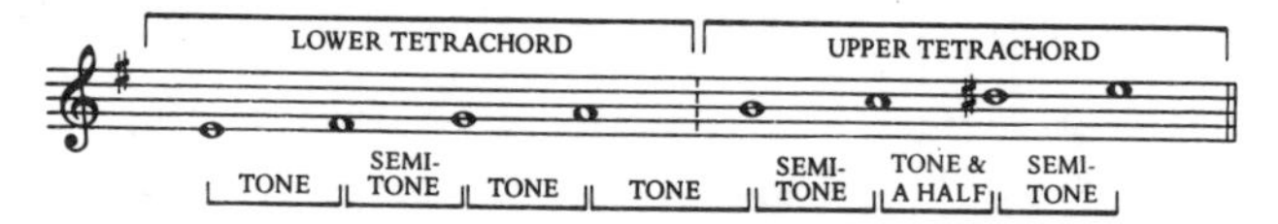

To form the melodic scale of E minor, we take the modal scale and, when ascending, sharpen the sixth and seventh notes by means of accidentals; when descending, we restore these notes to their original pitch (i.e. the notes of the modal minor scale).

Example 6.18

Scale of E Minor – Melodic Form

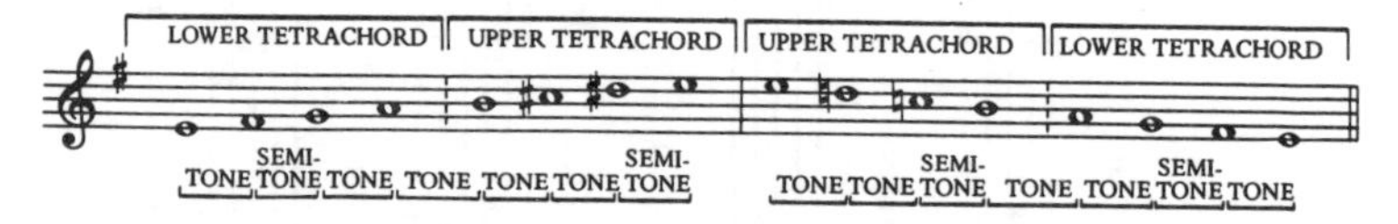

Continuing the process, we may form the other minor scales which have sharps in their key-signatures: B minor, F sharp minor,

C sharp minor, G sharp minor, D sharp minor and A sharp minor. (Although you will not be playing music in some of these keys until you are a very advanced player, you should study the *structure* of the scales in your scale book, and write them in your music book.)

The 'flat' series of minor scales is formed by taking the *lower* tetrachord of a modal minor scale, and adding a tetrachord *below* it. The tonic of one key thus becomes the dominant of another, so that the order goes *down* in fifths. But to form the pattern of the new upper tetrachord (semitone–tone–tone), we must *modify* the pattern of the old (lower) tetrachord. Thus, when taking the lower tetrachord of the modal A minor scale, and adding a tetrachord below it to form the modal D minor scale, we add a key-signature of one flat, which produces a semitone between the fifth and sixth degrees of the scale.

Example 6.19

Modal Scale of D Minor

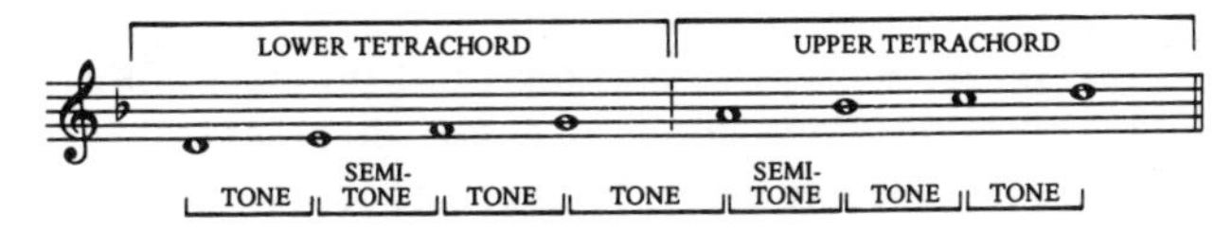

From the modal scale of D minor, we can form the harmonic scale of D minor, by sharpening the seventh note by means of an accidental.

Example 6.20

Scale of D Minor – Harmonic Form

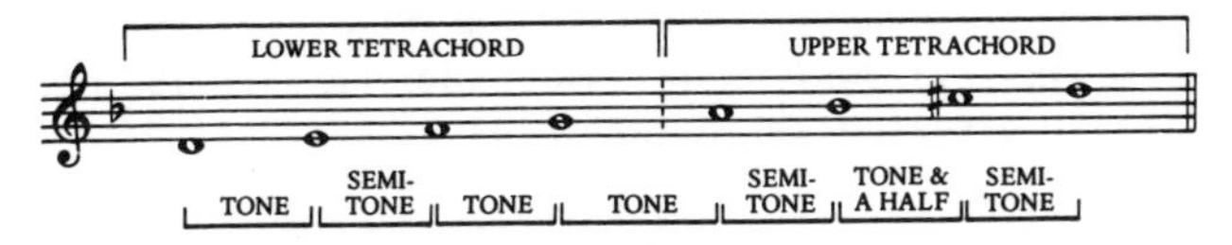

We can also form the melodic scale of D minor by sharpening the sixth and seventh notes of the modal scale, by means of accidentals, when ascending, and by restoring these notes to their original pitch when descending (Example 6.21).

Example 6.21

Scale of D Minor – Melodic Form

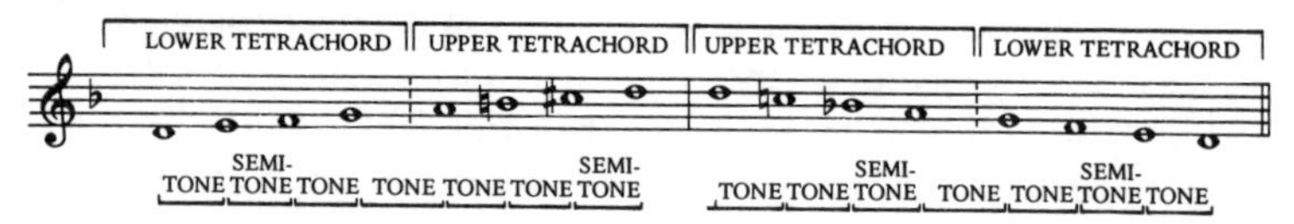

By the same process we can form the other minor scales which have flats in their key-signatures: G minor, C minor, F minor, B flat minor, E flat minor and A flat minor. (You should now study the structure of these scales in your scale book, and write them in your music book.)

In the early stages you will, of course, practise only a few of these scales, but it is important that you should understand the general principles of scale formation, which are often misunderstood, and it is for this reason that we have gone into the matter in some detail.

The chromatic scale

The *chromatic scale* consists entirely of semitones. Each octave contains twelve different notes arranged in alphabetical order, though there may be two notes of the same letter name: C and C sharp, D and D flat, and so on. On the piano, all the keys, white and black, are used in order.

The chromatic scale is usually formed by taking the notes of a major scale and 'filling in' the missing semitones, by adding sharps (or naturals) to sharpen notes in ascending, and by adding flats (or naturals) to flatten them in descending. (There are other methods of writing the chromatic scale. Example 8.11 (page 71) shows a different way of writing a chromatic scale starting on D.) Example 6.22 shows the chromatic scale starting on C. The white-headed notes are those of the C major scale; the black-headed notes are those added to form the chromatic scale.

Example 6.22

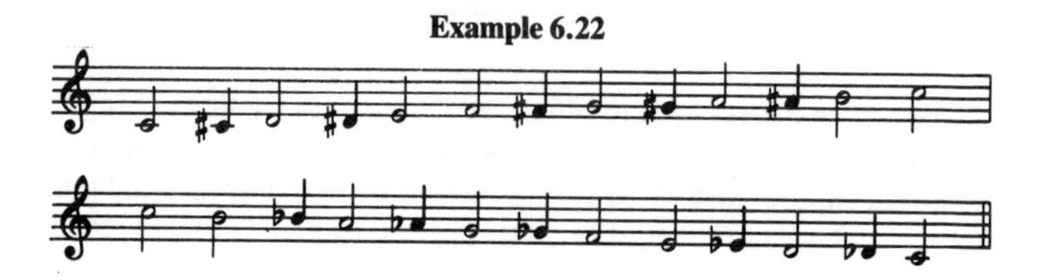

Double-sharps and double-flats

The pitch of a note which has already been sharpened or flattened may be raised or lowered by a semitone, if a *double-sharp* sign (𝄪), or a *double-flat* sign (♭♭) is placed immediately before the note. A double-sharp or double-flat may be reduced to a single sharp or flat by using the signs (♮♯) or (♮♭); of the note may be raised or lowered a tone, by using a *double-natural* sign (♮♮). Alternatively, the signs for a single sharp, flat, or natural may be used.

Example 6.23

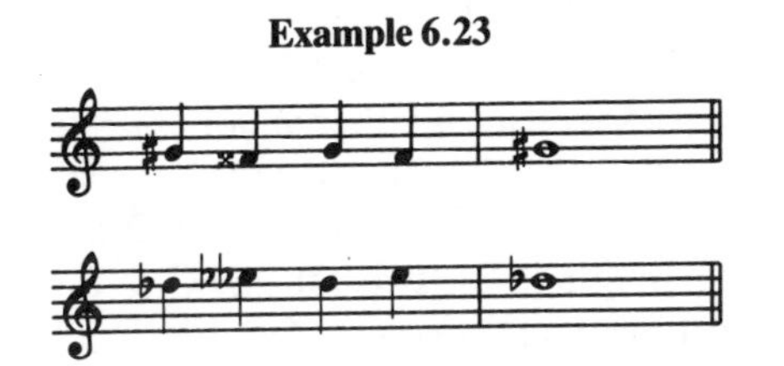

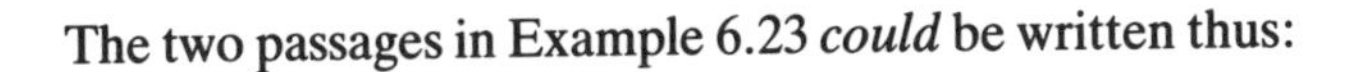

The two passages in Example 6.23 *could* be written thus:

Example 6.24

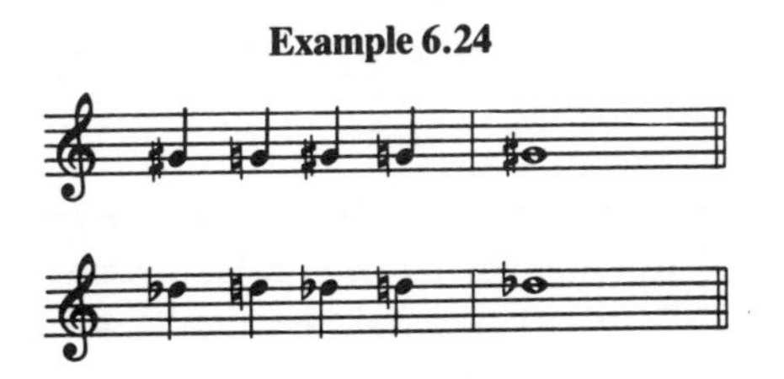

It is often convenient, however, to use double-sharps or double-flats to reduce the number of single flats, sharps and naturals which would otherwise be required. It should be noted that double-sharps and double-flats make it possible for each note of the scale to have three different letter names. Thus C, B sharp and D double-flat are enharmonics (see page 34), as are C sharp, D flat and B double-sharp; D, E double-flat and C double-sharp; and so on.

Intervals

The smallest interval, the semitone, or half-tone, is called *diatonic* when the two notes have different names (e.g. B and C), and *chromatic* when the two notes have the same letter names (e.g. C and C sharp). Intervals can be formed on any note of the scale, but the size of an interval depends on the number of tones and semitones which are included. Thus, the intervals B to C (a diatonic semitone) and B to C sharp (a tone) are both classified as 'seconds', though, as we shall see, one is a minor second and the other a major second.

An interval is calculated by counting the letter names upwards from the lower note to the higher,[1] both letter names being included in the total – thus C to F is a fourth, C to A a sixth, and so on.

Any interval which is counted from the first note of a major scale to any other note of that scale is either *major* or *perfect*. It is useful to relate intervals to the piano keyboard, and to observe the number of tones and semitones in each interval. C to D is a major second (tone); C to E a major third (two tones); C to F a perfect fourth (two-and-a-half-tones), and so on.

Example 6.25

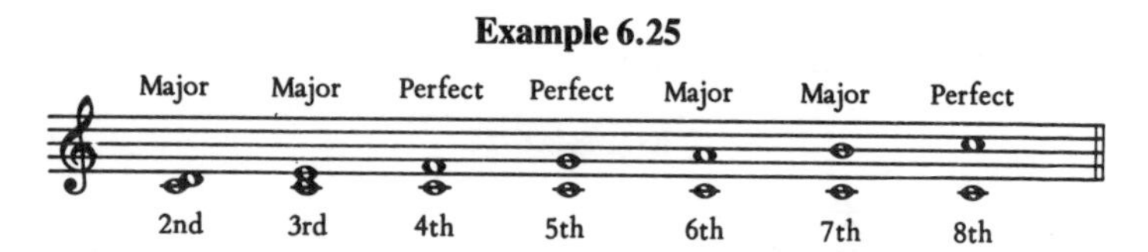

If a major interval is reduced by a semitone (by flattening the upper note or sharpening the lower note) it becomes *minor*. Thus C to E flat, or C sharp to E natural, are minor thirds. A perfect or major interval, if increased by a semitone, becomes *augmented* (e.g. C to D sharp, and C flat to D natural are augmented seconds). A perfect or minor interval, if decreased by a semitone, becomes *diminished* (e.g. C to G flat, and C sharp to G natural are diminished fifths).

Note that, as intervals are calculated by counting the letter names *upwards*, two intervals having identical pitch but different letter names may be differently described. Thus, C to F sharp is an

[1] An interval which exceeds the compass of an octave is said to be *compound* (i.e. a *simple* interval to which an octave has been added). A compound interval can be reduced to a simple interval by subtracting seven (e.g. a ninth ($9-7=2$) can be reduced to a second). Compound intervals are calculated by counting letter names upwards (e.g. C to E (three notes above) is a major third; C to E (ten notes above) is a major tenth).

augmented fourth, but C to G flat, a diminished fifth; C to E flat is a minor third, but C to D sharp, an augmented second, and so on.

An interval may be *inverted* by playing either the top note an octave lower, or the bottom note an octave higher. Perfect intervals, when inverted, remain perfect; minor intervals become major; augmented intervals become diminished, and diminished intervals augmented.

Chords

Chords are combinations of notes which are sounded together.

Example 6.26

The simplest kind of chord can be formed by taking any note of the scale, which we will call the bass or *root*, and adding two other notes above it, one a third and the other a fifth from the root. The chord so formed is called a *triad*. Triads can be formed on any degree of the major or minor scale using only the notes of the scale itself.

Triads formed on the degrees of a major scale can be of three kinds:

(a) *Major:* with the two upper notes a major third and a perfect fifth from the root.
(b) *Minor:* with the two upper notes a minor third and a perfect fifth from the root.
(c) *Diminished:* with the two upper notes a minor third and a diminished fifth from the root.

Example 6.27

Key of C Major

Major Minor Minor Major Major Minor Diminished

I II III IV V VI VII

Triads formed on the degrees of a minor scale include, in addition to major, minor and diminished triads, an augmented triad on the third degree, with the two upper notes a major third and an augmented fifth from the root.

Example 6.28

Key of A Minor

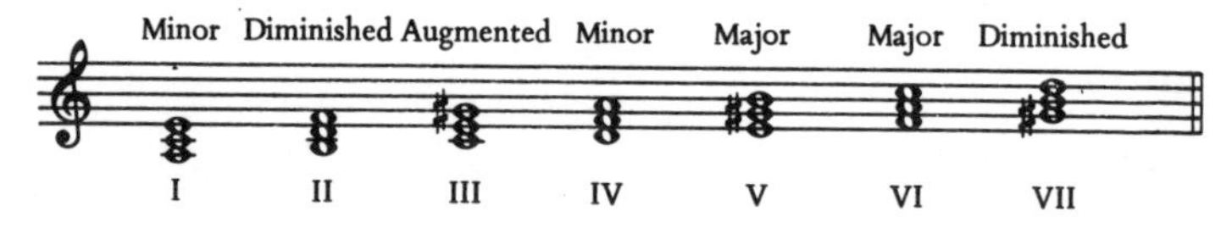

If you play the triads in Examples 6.27 and 6.28, you will probably feel that both major and minor triads sound complete in themselves, but that diminished and augmented triads sound incomplete until they are resolved upon major or minor chords.[1]

Example 6.29

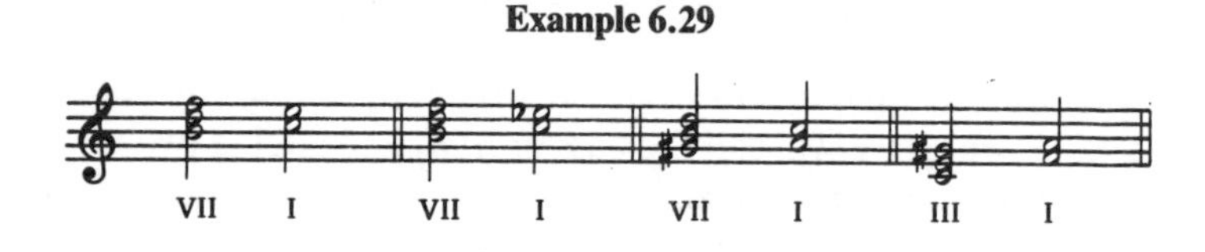

Arpeggios and broken chords

Arpeggios are chords, the notes of which instead of being sounded together are played one after the other.

Broken chords are similar to *arpeggios*, except that the notes are played out of order.

Example 6.30

[1] Although a chord is, properly, three or more notes sounded together, the two-note intervals in Example 6.29 can, in the context, be regarded as incomplete major or minor triads.

Self-testing questions

(Please see Preliminary remarks in Chapter 3, page 15.)

1 What is an interval? (*See page 32*)
2 (a) What is a scale? (b) Which two seven-note 'modal' scales have survived in modern music? (c) What are these two scales sometimes called? (*See pages 32–3*)
3 Which adjacent white piano keys are (a) a tone apart; (b) a semitone apart? (*See page 31*)
4 Write the Roman Numerals which refer to the 'degrees' of the scale, and against each numeral write the name of the degree. (*See page 33, and Example 6.1*)
5 Name (a) the 'ruling' note of the scale; (b) the 'governing' note of the scale; (c) the note which tends to lead to the tonic. (*See page 33*)
6 What is the effect of placing before a natural note (a) a sharp sign; (b) a flat sign? (*See pages 34–5, and Example 6.2*)
7 Write, on the treble stave, the notes C sharp and D flat. (*Example 6.2*)
8 Which notes on the piano, when sharpened or flattened, are played on the white keys? (*See page 34*)
9 Each piano black key may be represented as either a sharp note or a flat note. Give alternative names for (a) C sharp; (b) G flat; (c) B flat; (d) D sharp; (e) G sharp. (*Example 6.3*)
10 Write, on the treble stave, the notes F sharp and G flat. Show how these notes may be restored to their 'natural' pitch. (*Example 6.4*)
11 What are 'accidentals', and which notes do they affect? (*See page 34*)
12 What is a tetrachord? (*See page 36*)
13 Write the scale of C major (one octave, treble clef), marking the tones and semitones which make up each tetrachord. Name the interval which joins the tetrachords together. (*Example 6.7*)
14 Show how the scale of G major can be formed on the same pattern. Put a sharp before the note which much be raised in pitch. (*Example 6.8*)
15 Write the key-signature of the scale of G major. (*Example 6.9*)
16 Write the scale of D major (one octave, treble clef), with the correct key-signature. (*Example 6.10*)
17 Write the key-signature and scale of F major (one octave, treble clef). (*Example 6.11*)
18 Which piano keys represent the modal scale of A minor? (*See page 30*)
19 Write the modal scale of A minor. (*Example 6.12*)
20 Write the scale of A minor (harmonic form). (*Example 6.13*)
21 Write the scale of A minor (melodic form). (*Example 6.14*)
22 What does a major scale have in common with its *tonic* minor? (*See page 40*)
23 What does a major scale have in common with its *relative* minor? (*See page 40*)
24 Write the key-signatures of these scales, naming the relative minor of

each: (a) A major; (b) F major; (c) G major; (d) A flat major; (e) B major; (f) D flat major. (*Example 6.15*)

25 Write the modal scale of E minor. (*Example 6.16*)
26 Write the scale of E minor (harmonic form). (*Example 6.17*)
27 Write the scale of E minor (melodic form). (*Example 6.18*)
28 Write the modal scale of D minor. (*Example 6.19*)
29 Write the scale of D minor (harmonic form). (*Example 6.20*)
30 Write the scale of D minor (melodic form). (*Example 6.21*)
31 Write the chromatic scale starting on Middle C (one octave, ascending and descending). (*Example 6.22*)
32 What effect has (a) a double-sharp; (b) a double-flat? What are the signs for these? What signs reduce double-sharps and double-flats to single ones? (*See pages 45–6, and Examples 6.23 and 6.24*)
33 Write the intervals of a major scale, marking each 'perfect' or 'major'. (*Example 6.25*)
34 What is (a) a chord; (b) a triad? (*See page 47*)
35 Write the triads in the key of C major, marking each 'major', 'minor', or 'diminished'. (*Example 6.27*)
36 Write the triads in the key of A minor, marking each 'major', 'minor', 'diminished', or 'augmented'. (*Example 6.28*)
37 Which triads sound complete in themselves, and which sound incomplete until resolved upon major or minor chords? (*See page 49, and Example 6.29*)
38 Write in the key of C major (a) an *arpeggio*; (b) a broken chord. (*Example 6.30*)

7

How to Practise

Any readers who may aspire to become professional concert pianists will probably have realised that they will have to find an outstanding teacher, and follow his (or her) advice. The road to virtuosity is long and hard, demanding not only a high degree of inborn talent, but also the ability and desire to devote many hours a day to soul-searching practice and study, in the burning pursuit of a goal which may, in the end, prove elusive.

If you are playing the piano purely for your own pleasure (and possibly that of some others) careful practice is still essential if you wish to make real progress; but when music is a part-time creative (or re-creative) activity, practice will necessarily be on a more limited scale. We need not therefore devote much space to 'over-practice' which, for the would-be virtuoso, may sometimes result in strained fingers and hands, and is a waste of physical and nervous energy.

However, even short periods of 'aimless' practice may, instead of proving beneficial, serve only to develop and perpetuate faults. Properly directed practice is therefore of first importance and can transform periods of drudgery into periods of enlightenment.

If you are doing other work during the day, you may find that the only time you are able to set aside for practice is when you are not feeling at your best. If you have real enthusiasm for the piano this should not be too much of a problem, but a few general guidelines may be of help.

In the early stages of piano playing, hands and arms will be subjected to unfamiliar sequences of muscular exertion, and periods of practice should be quite short. As muscles become stronger practice periods may be extended gradually, so long as a break is made whenever hands, arms or mind begin to feel tired or tense. It is worthwhile, now and again, taking the hands from the keyboard, and letting the arms fall limply to the sides for a few moments, so that any stiffness and tension are relieved. In longer periods complete changes of body posture are essential from time to time. These can be combined with some small mental or physical relaxation or enjoyment – a walk around the room, a cup of tea, reading a book for a few minutes, for example.

There may be times when playing something will provide solace from grief or disappointment, or relief from anger or frustration, but attempts to practise under conditions of stress, or great tiredness, are not usually rewarding. Practising is, of course, a highly individual experience, and your personal approach is therefore of great importance. If you are studying on your own, or with minimal help from a teacher, you may feel the lack of encouragement and support which every good teacher ought to offer. Nevertheless, you must be reasonably optimistic about your prospects, however small. Those who say 'I can't do it' never can, unless and until they are persuaded otherwise.

One of the disappointments of practising, especially for the mature adult beginner, is that at times progress appears to be non-existent, and when things seem to be getting worse instead of better, the would-be pianist begins to wonder whether he, or she, really has the necessary talent for even the most modest achievements. Progress, however, is seldom a continuous process of advancement, but rather a matter of 'three steps forward and two backwards'. It is important to recognise this *before* discouragement sets in, and to see the problem in its right perspective. Compare today's performance with yesterday's, and you may decide that today's careful practice has been a waste of time. But perhaps yesterday's mood was more perceptive (or your energy cycle more active). Compare today's performance with that of a week or a month ago, and your true progress may be more apparent.

Although 'aimless' practice is to be avoided, it is often a mistake to set yourself too rigid a target or timetable. Ten minutes scale practice, timed with a stop watch, is likely to be less useful than the resolve to practise a single scale for as long as the undertaking seems to be worthwhile, and you are able to give it undivided care and attention. It is usually undesirable to practise one thing for a very long time to the exclusion of everything else, though this may sometimes be necessary for examination purposes. Also, it is usually desirable to have two or more pieces in progress at a time, preferably in contrasted styles. Occasionally, it may be good to have a 'playing' of anything and everything which takes your fancy (including piano duets if you can find a partner) simply for your personal pleasure and amusement.

Before starting to practise, try to have a clear idea of what you are going to do. If you start a technical exercise without understanding *why* you are playing it, you will not be able to identify and correct any faults which may occur. And if you are studying an unfamiliar piece, you will not get far if you fail to observe the key- and time-signatures. Everything you play – scales, *arpeggios*, pieces, studies, sight-reading – needs to be prepared in the mind before you start. 'If you don't know, don't go', says a manual on car driving. Or, in the words of Liszt, 'Think ten times and play once!'. Concentration, interest, observation and listening are the essential ingredients of worthwhile practice.

Finding the key of a piece

It is not always easy to decide the key of a piece of music, simply by looking at the key-signature. A movement, for example, with two sharps in the key-signature could be in either D major or B minor, since both keys share the same key-signature. As a general rule the last lowest note in the left hand will usually be the key-note.[1] Thus, in Example 7.1 the final note in the left hand is B, and the piece is in B minor.

In easier piano music, the final note in the left hand will almost invariably be the key-note, but accidentals may often provide useful clues. For example, a melody with a key-signature without sharps or flats could be in C major or in A minor. In C major, one would

[1] 'Key-note' is used in preference to 'tonic', because this term is used by The Associated Board, and other leading bodies, in connection with aural tests, etc.

Example 7.1

Prelude *Chopin*
Op.28, No. 6

expect to find G naturals in the melody, as in Example 7.2(a). If sharps appear, it is likely that these are accidentally sharpened leading notes in the key of A minor, and that the piece is in that key, as in Example 7.2(b).

Example 7.2

Experience in hearing and analysing phrases before playing them will help you identify a key with some confidence.

What to look for

Before studying a new piece, always look through the music slowly and carefully, taking note of anything which may help you to understand it. What is the name of the composer, his nationality, and when did he live? What is the style and character of the music? Is it romantic, grave or gay? And is there a description which may help (nocturne, minuet, etc.)? You should not play Bach like Beethoven, still less like Debussy. Look at the phrasing, cadences and so on, and try to get as complete a mental picture as possible of how the piece should sound.

It may be useful to number the bars (lightly in pencil which can be rubbed out later); then, from time to time, you can write down the numbers of those bars which present special difficulties, and the nature of these; you can then practise these bars separately, making notes of your progress. (To save time, you could number every fifth bar.)

The first essential is accuracy – correct notes, time-values, fingering, and so on. Until you can play with reasonable accuracy, you cannot really begin to interpret the thoughts of the composer. So, begin by isolating difficult passages one by one as you go along, correcting faults before they become habits. Consider phrasing. Singing over passages will help you to appreciate the shape of the phrases, how the music moves along, and where cadences and climaxes occur. What kind of finger technique will you use, and where, if at all, might the sustaining pedal be appropriate?

It is a great help if you can memorise some of the music, even if, at first, you are able to remember only a few bars at a time. This applies particularly to the opening bars of a piece; if you know them by heart, you will be able to give your complete attention to your playing – to watch your hands, to judge the appropriate tone level, and so on. It will also help you to make a good start when you are playing at a performance or examination, and thus to feel more confidence in your ability.

When practising, however, do not fall into the habit of *always* starting at the beginning. The opening bars may be the easiest, and more time may need to be spent on difficult bars. It is better to isolate phrases (usually of two or four bars) which need most attention, and to concentrate on these. Of course you should also play the piece right through from time to time. Sometimes it is useful to start in the middle of a piece and play to the end; or even to start with the last phrase, and work backwards phrase by phrase. It is important that you should be able to begin at *any* bar.

Counting time

In order to give each note or rest exactly the right duration of sound or silence, you must learn to count time accurately. When practising, it is helpful, particularly in the early stages, to count aloud. You may not find this easy, but it will come with practice, and audible counting will enable you to establish the shape and phrasing of the music, as well as to keep in correct time. Time is usually counted by the number of beats in each bar. In a bar of $\frac{2}{4}$, $\frac{3}{4}$ or $\frac{4}{4}$ time, for example, each beat is represented by one crotchet or its equivalent (see Example 5.9), and each crotchet (or its equivalent) is therefore counted as one beat:

Example 7.3

From Example 7.3 you will see that two quavers (= one crotchet) are counted as one beat, and one minim (= two crotchets) as two beats. If, however, the music is slow, you could subdivide each crotchet into two half-beats, calling the second half-beat 'and'.

Example 7.4

To a Wild Rose (Woodland Sketches) — *MacDowell*
Op. 15, No. 1

Although, when this piece is being learnt, you will find it useful to count '1 and 2 and' throughout, when you know the music really well, and can sing the whole phrase from memory, you should be able to 'think' in terms of: 1 and 2– 1 and 2– 1 and 2 and 1–2–, and so on.

Observe that in Example 7.4 there is no precise indication of speed, although 'with simple tenderness' suggests that the music is not fast, as does the expressive melody. The appropriate speed is of course a matter for individual feeling and judgement.

It is not always easy to decide the appropriate speed for a piece of music, and how to count it. The markings of the composer (sometimes very few, or even none at all) may give some indication: *adagio* means slow, but how slow?; *allegro* means lively, but how lively? Qualifying terms may also help: e.g. *adagio non troppo* (not too slow); *allegro assai* (very fast). In deciding the appropriate speed of a movement, start by looking right through it so that, first, you can be guided by the character and style of the whole movement, and secondly you can take into account the fastest passages. If the movement begins with crotchets and proceeds to semiquavers, the speed at which you will be able to play the semiquavers must be considered when deciding the overall speed.

It is always helpful to sing a melody which is being practised at the keyboard, and also to sing it away from the keyboard (e.g. in the bath); by doing so, the phrasing and general character will be made clearer.

A bar of $\frac{6}{8}$ time would normally be counted as two dotted crotchets.

Example 7.5

The Wild Horseman (Album for the Young) — *Schumann*
Op. 68, No. 8

If, however, the music is slow, a bar of $\frac{6}{8}$ time could be counted as six quavers.

Example 7.6

Romance from Sonatina in G — *Beethoven*

Similarly, a bar of $\frac{9}{8}$ or $\frac{12}{8}$ time could be counted either as three or four dotted crotchets, or as nine or twelve quavers.

Where triplets occur, each group of three should be counted as one.

Example 7.7

Minuet in F *Mozart*

The metronome

This is a clock-like instrument which has a flat steel pendulum which swings from side to side with a click; variations of speed are obtained by moving an adjustable weight up and down the pendulum. A graduated scale behind the pendulum covers a range from about 40 to 208 ticks (or beats) to the minute.

Sometimes a metronome marking is added by the composer (or music editor), to indicate the speed at which the music should be played. Thus, ♩ = 120 means that if the weight is placed opposite 120 on the scale, the metronome will give 120 ticks to the minute, and that each crotchet has the value of one tick. Metronome marks are not always to be relied on; for example, in the works of some composers, such as Schumann and Grieg, they should not be taken too literally.

Apart from indicating the speed of a piece of music, the metronome may sometimes be a useful aid when practising; if it is left ticking while you are playing, any deviation from the beat should be evident. It is seldom advisable to keep the metronome ticking for long periods, however, as mechanical time-keeping is no substitute for a sense of rhythm, and constant reliance on the 'tick' is likely to weaken rhythmic feeling.

Intensity and speed

Words, abbreviations and signs which indicate the relative intensity of sounds are called dynamics: for example *piano* (*p*) = soft, *forte* (*f*) = loud, *crescendo* (*cres.* or <) = increasing in volume, *decrescendo* or *diminuendo* (*decresc* or *dim*, or >) = decreasing in volume (see Glossary of terms, page 144).

The dynamic range will vary according to the period of the music. In much early music there are no original dynamic indications, and although these are often added to printed music by modern editors, they are only in the nature of suggestions. Up to Beethoven's time, *pianissimo (pp)* and *fortissimo (ff)* were usually taken to mean 'as soft' or 'as loud' as possible. Since Beethoven's time, some composers have increased the range to *ppp, fff,* or even *pppp,* etc. This must be taken into account when playing music for the older keyboard instruments (including early pianos); since these instruments were not capable of nearly such a wide dynamic range as the modern piano; the range of dynamics when playing Mozart, for example, will be quite different from the range when playing Liszt or Debussy.

Dynamics need to be carefully thought out. If, for instance, a *forte* is followed by a *piano*, the level of tone must be such that a satisfactory contrast is produced. In Example 7.8, *forte* tone must be maintained throughout the first bar, and there must be a *sudden* drop to *piano* at the beginning of the second bar.

Example 7.8

Sonata No. 14 in D Major *Haydn*

Crescendos and *diminuendos* need to be well planned, especially if they extend over a number of bars, so that they are made gradually, and not exhausted so quickly that a level tone is reached too soon, instead of continuing the rise or fall. The sign >, or the words *sforzando* (*sf*) or *forzato* (*fz*) (It. literally, 'forcing') indicate that the note or chord so marked is to be strongly emphasised with an accent. It is important, however, that the strength of the accent should be related to the passage in which it occurs; in a *forte* passage, it is obvious that the accent will have to be far heavier than in a *piano* passage.

Variations of speed, such as *accelerando* (*accel*) = quickening the pace, or *rallentando* (*rall*) or *ritenuto* (*rit*) = slowing down, also need to be carefully planned, so that the increase or decrease in speed is made gradually, according to the speed of the music, and the length of the phrase involved.

Training the ear

Critical listening is the basis of all good piano playing, and at least a few minutes (say three or four times a week) should be devoted to ear-training. The books of aural tests published for grade examinations held by The Associated Board and other examining bodies may be used for practice. For some of these tests, you will need to enlist the help of a musical friend to play for you, but there are several tests that you can practise on your own.[1]

1 Close your eyes, and play a note at random on the piano, keeping your finger on the key. Sing the note, and check the result by playing it again (try to keep within the range of your voice).
2 Play the key-chord and key-note[2] of a major scale. Choose, at random, any note of the scale (2nd, 3rd, 4th, etc.) and sing it, checking the result by playing it. Example 7.9 shows the procedure.

Example 7.9

Scale of D Major

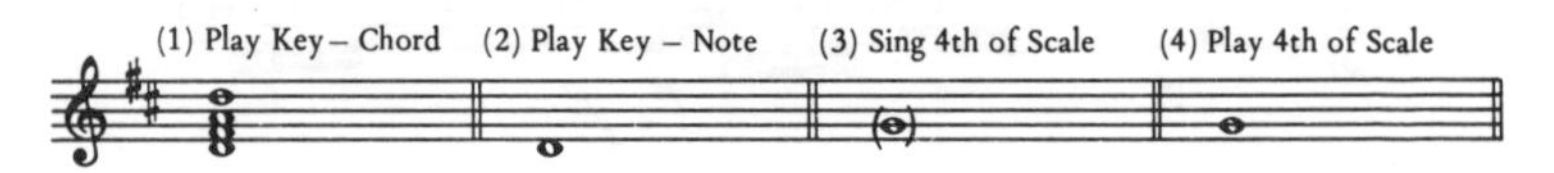

At first you may find that you need to sing up from the key-note to the fourth note, as in Example 7.10.

[1] Alternatively, there are aural cassettes available, one for each Grade 1–8, from Sound Wise, 23 Frithville Gardens, London W12 7JG.
[2] Key-chord = the major triad formed on the key-note (see page 33).

Example 7.10

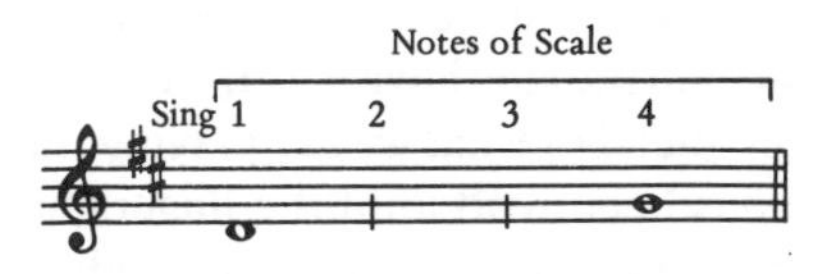

As soon as possible, however, try to 'think' up the first three notes of the scale, singing only the fourth note. Later, with practice, you should be able to think from the key-note directly to the note you have to sing.

3 From the test book play two notes together (i.e. a two-part interval). Describe the interval (major third, perfect fifth, etc.), and check by counting letter names from the lower note to the higher, etc. (see page 46).
4 From the test book, play a short melodic phrase twice, having first played the key-chord. Sing the phrase, and check by playing it again.
5 From the test book, sing at sight a group of three or more related notes (or a short melodic phrase), having first played the key-chord and key-note, but *not* the phrase. Check by playing the phrase. Simple melodies (folk tunes and hymns, etc.) can also be used for sight-singing.
6 From the test book, play a short melodic phrase twice and clap the rhythm. Check by playing the phrase again. Also clap the rhythm *before* playing it. (This does, of course, presume that you are able to play the phrase *accurately*.)
7 Sing from memory a short melodic phrase from a piece you are studying, then try to write it in your music book. Check with the printed copy. (If necessary, look at the key, and play the key-note on the piano before you start.)

Sight-reading

Sight-reading is to some extent a natural gift; certainly it presents fewer problems to some pianists than to others, even though the latter may be the more accomplished pianists. Those who find sight-reading difficult may, however, develop what ability they have to a reasonable standard by intelligent and regular practice.

Sight-reading is first a matter of observation; the eyes must take in clefs, time- and key-signatures, notes, phrasing, dynamics, and so on. Then, the fingers must make the appropriate response to what the eyes have read, and the ears have heard. And since we must read at least a few notes ahead of what we are playing, the memory must then retain what has been read until the fingers have translated it into sound. In addition, the sight-reader must judge the appropriate speed, style, and interpretation of the music.

Although, in normal practice, it is often useful to be able to watch the hands (having memorised the music to be played), with sight-reading this is not possible. It follows that you must be able to find notes on the piano easily and accurately, without having to glance down at your fingers. Practising scales or short phrases with closed eyes (or with the fingers on top of the closed piano cover), can be useful; also naming a note at random, and trying to find it on the keyboard without looking. The 'feel' of a chord can also be memorised by placing the fingers on the keys, lifting them, and then trying to play the chord with the eyes closed.

When sight-reading from printed music, start quite slowly and try to play strictly in time. Instead of stopping each time you make a mistake (as we all do sometimes), return to the places where the mistakes occurred *after* you have finished the movement, and meanwhile try to carry on calmly.

Instead of thinking of the name of each note, try to hear the sound it represents; this may not be easy at first, but practice in reading through music *before* playing it is a great help. Try also to understand the harmonic and melodic pattern of the music. Watch for *cadences* (see Chapter 10) and sequences. (A *sequence* is a more or less exact repetition of a melody (with or without harmony), at a higher or lower pitch, as in Example 7.11.)

Example 7.11

Remember to look as far ahead as you can, so that the grouping and phrasing of the notes is apparent, and there is a feeling of the music 'going somewhere'. Difficult chords may have to be read upwards from the lowest note.

Demonstration Lesson Three gives detailed advice about sight-reading, and should be studied with care.

Memorising music

Memory implies two things: the capacity to retain knowledge, and the power to recall it. The accuracy with which we retain knowledge depends on how deeply it interests and impresses us; an association of ideas also helps us to remember.

Memory for music depends on three forms of perception: visual, aural and tactile. Some people have great powers of visual perception, and are able to see a page of music in the mind's eye. Those who do not possess this 'photographic' memory will find that music is easier to visualise if the complete shape is concentrated on, before the music is analysed in detail. Points to look for are (a) the pattern or the melody, harmony and fingering; (b) passages, if any, which are repeated, either exactly or in sequence; (c) passages which are based on familiar figures, such as scales, broken chords, or *arpeggios*. Writing out music (a few bars at a time) is often a useful aid to memory.

Aural perception enables the ear to take in the general 'design' of the music as well as the details. It can be developed by careful ear-training and listening. Tactile perception means that the pianist is able to memorise the *feel* of the fingers as they play. Practice with closed eyes (as recommended in the previous section on sight-reading) will help to develop this faculty (scales and *arpeggios* should be included).

Since nervousness often makes memorising difficult and causes memory failure, it is wise to avoid too much conscious effort; at times it is better to read or play music through, noting the various points, without *trying* to memorise it.

It is often also helpful to break up the music into small parts, perhaps even a bar or two at a time. First look at the notes in the right hand, and name them aloud. Now close your eyes, and try to 'imagine' these notes; then, with the eyes still closed, play them five times. Repeat with your left hand, and finally with both hands together. This procedure takes time, but may bring rewarding results.

Some final points

If you know a pianist of approximately the same ability as yourself, try to arrange some duet-playing. There is a large selection of music for four hands at one piano, some of it quite easy. Duet-playing is enjoyable and it is also valuable as an exercise in sight-reading and time-keeping, and for the exchange of ideas with other pianists.

Opportunities of playing before an audience should be welcomed, even if it consists of one or two friends only. They will help you to acquire self-confidence, particularly if you are apprehensive about appearing before an examiner in grade examinations (though you will find that he, or she, is quite human, and will try to put you at ease).

The cassette (or tape) recorder also offers unique opportunities for self-criticism. By playing back your recordings of pieces, studies, scales, and so on, you can not only note your weak points, but also the progress you have made since your previous recording.

Most of your practice periods should include written work. Scales, *arpeggios*, chords, and so on are much more easily understood and remembered if you write them in your music book before playing them. It is also good practice (and fun) to compose and play short melodies. At first, these could be phrases consisting of a few notes; based, perhaps, on suitable words (e.g. FADE, DEAF, BEAD).

Finally, no one should *have* to practise except, perhaps, the very young. Practice is seldom worthwhile unless it is undertaken willingly, and for good reasons – to improve technique and interpretation, to prepare for performance and examination, to provide a yardstick with which to measure progress, and encouragement to go further. Given real desire to learn to play, the necessary self-discipline will follow.

8

Fingering

Printed fingering

Most piano music has fingering marked, and you are advised to avoid unfingered music, especially in the early stages. Printed fingering, however, is intended for pianists with average-sized hands, and if, after trying the suggested fingering for a reasonable period, you find that some of it does not suit you, do not hesitate to alter it. Methods of fingering have changed over the years. Once, for example, the use of the thumb on black keys was not allowed, but it is now freely used in passage work. The development of *legato* pedalling has also resulted in changes of fingering, so that music by Bach, if played without pedal, may be fingered differently from music by Chopin or Debussy.

When playing scales and exercises, it is best to use printed fingering where possible, as it is usually devised with a special purpose in mind, but alternative fingerings are sometimes possible. When music has little or no fingering marked, work out the most simple fingering you can (the easiest is usually the best). Once you have decided on the fingering, try to memorise it and stick to it. Some pianists confuse themselves by using different fingering each time they play, thus making accurate performance almost impossible.

The principles of fingering

The basic principles of fingering are not difficult to understand. In a passage of five consecutive notes, played on the white keys, the five fingers are used in order. (In the examples which follow, the fingering above the notes is for the right hand, and that below the notes for the left hand.)

Example 8.1

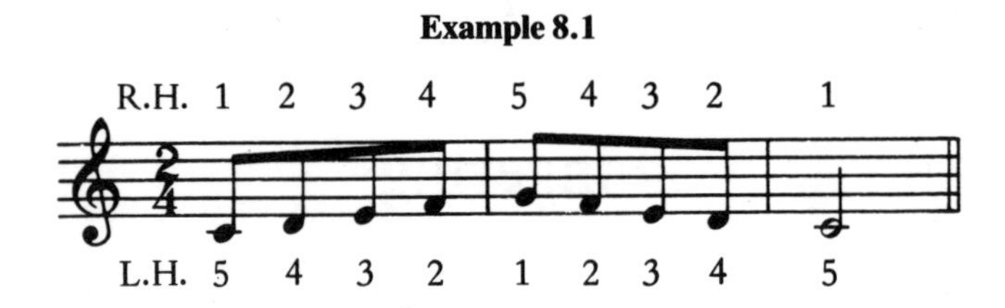

In a passage which lies under the hand (i.e. which does not exceed a five-note span), when any white note is left out, the finger which would play that note is also left out.

Example 8.2

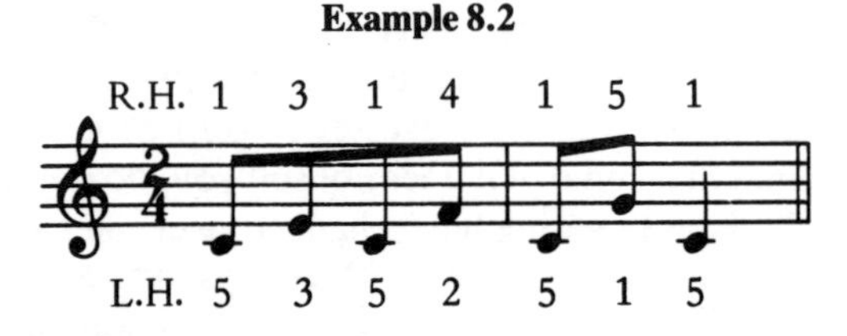

Passages exceeding five consecutive white notes are fingered by passing the thumb under the fingers, or the fingers over the thumb.

Example 8.3

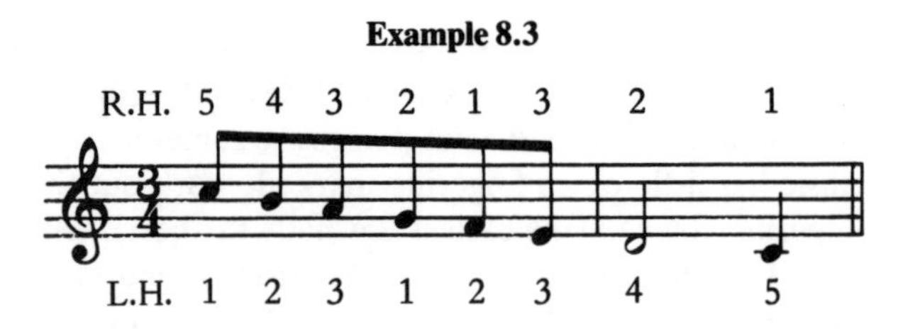

Note patterns

Sequences (groups of notes forming a pattern which is repeated higher up, or lower down, the keyboard) may often be fingered alike.

Example 8.4

The fingers are sometimes contracted to allow one or more fingers to be omitted, so that a passage will lie more easily under the hand. Thus, in Example 8.5, in which both upper and lower parts are played by the right hand, the fourth finger is followed by the second, even though these consecutive notes are only a tone apart.[1]

Example 8.5

For similar reasons, fingers are often extended or stretched. In Example 8.6, consecutive notes, a third apart, are taken by the second and fourth (and by the fourth and fifth, and second and first) fingers of the right hand, and by the third and second (and by the second and first, and third and fifth) fingers of the left hand. Consecutive notes a fourth apart are taken by the first and second fingers of the right hand, and by the fifth and third fingers of the left hand.

Example 8.6

[1] When two parts are played by the same hand, as in Examples 8.5 and 8.7, the upper and lower figures indicate fingering relating, respectively, to the upper and lower parts.

Looking again at Example 8.5, you will see that the first finger is used for each of the two consecutive notes in the lower part. Although, because of this, it is not possible to play the two lower notes absolutely smoothly and without a break, this is compensated for by the smoothness of the melody in the upper part.

Changing fingers on the same note

In Example 8.6, different fingers are used when the note G is repeated by the right and left hands. This device allows the hand to be shifted down (or up) the keyboard, and also allows the repeated notes to be neatly phrased. Sometimes, one finger may be substituted for another while a key is being held down, to obviate a break between notes or to allow a change of position in a passage.

Example 8.7

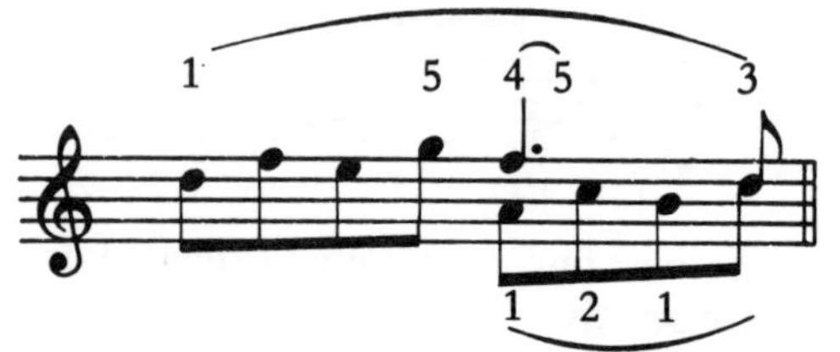

In Example 8.7, the fifth finger is substituted for the fourth (while the key is held down), the change being indicated by a bracket over the figures four and five.

It is sometimes convenient to use the same finger for repeated notes; on the other hand, although the practice of changing fingers is not so strictly adhered to as it used to be, it is often useful. In Example 8.8, the phrasing and shape of the melody is made clearer by the change of finger on the second D, and the fingering is made easier by the change of finger on the first note of the final group of four semiquavers.

Example 8.8

Example 8.9

Scale of C Major

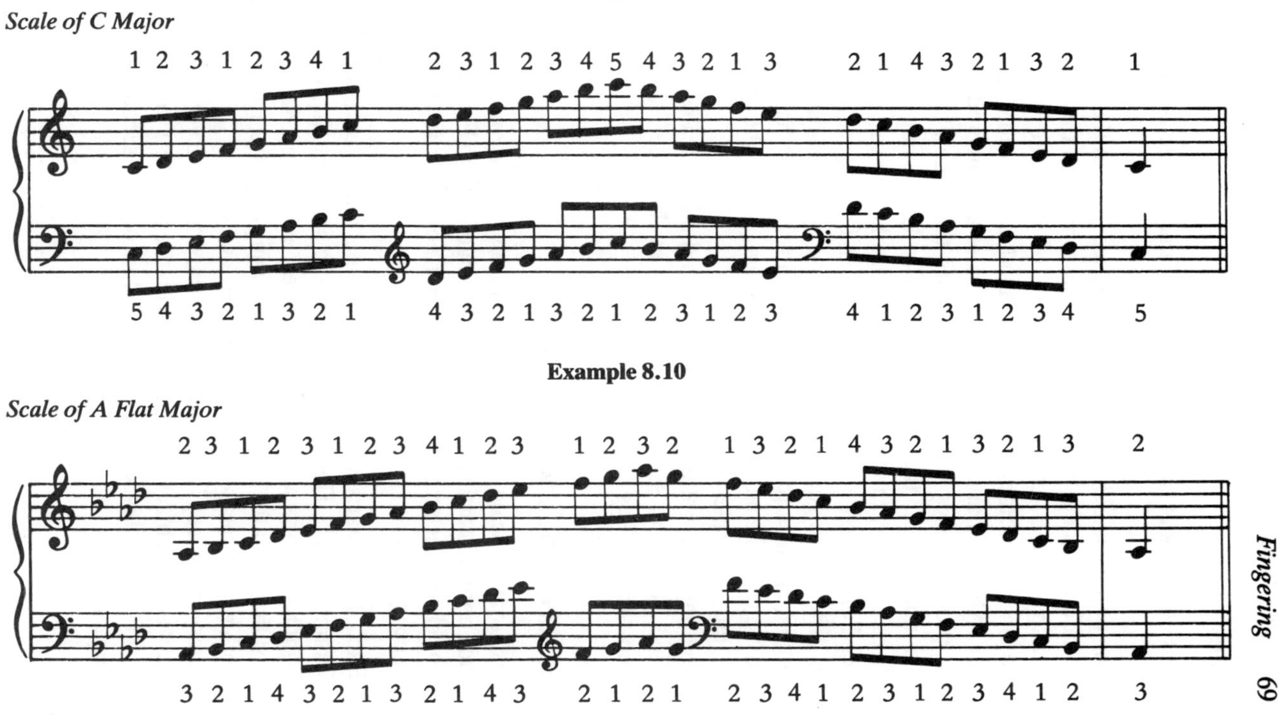

Example 8.10

Scale of A Flat Major

Scales

Let us now look at the fingering of the C major scale (see Example 8.9).

The pattern is 123, 1234, and so on (ascending in the right hand, descending in the left), or 4321 321 (descending in the right hand, ascending in the left). The top note of the scale in the right hand, and the bottom note in the left hand, are played with the fifth finger. All major and minor diatonic scales are fingered on similar principles, but they do not all start with the same fingers. Major and minor scales in the keys of G, D, A and E are fingered like the scale of C major, the thumbs coming together on the key-note, at the end of the first octave. Other major and minor scales may start with different fingers in each hand. The A flat major scale, for example, starts with the second finger in the right hand, and the third finger in the left. It does, nevertheless, follow the pattern 123, 1234, etc (Example 8.10).

The fingering patterns of all major and minor scales should be studied from your scale book, perhaps in the order suggested in Demonstration Lesson Two.

The chromatic scale

The chromatic scale, which consists entirely of semitones, may start on any note. If starting on D, it may be fingered as in Example 8.11.

For chromatic scales starting on other notes, the following rules may be applied:

1 Each hand starts with the appropriate finger, as indicated in Example 8.11. Thus, in the chromatic scale starting on C, the right hand starts with the second finger, and the left hand with the first finger. In the chromatic scale starting on A flat (or G sharp), both hands start with the third finger, and so on.
2 Every black key is played with the third finger. Every white key between two black keys is played with the thumb. Two white keys together are played with the first and second (or second and first) fingers.

Example 8.11

1 3 1 2 3 1 3 1 3 1 2 3 1 3 2 1 3 1 3 1 3 2 1 3 1
1 3 2 1 3 1 3 1 3 2 1 3 1 3 1 2 3 1 3 1 3 1 2 3 1

Example 8.12

Arpeggio of C major

(a)

1 2 3 1 2 3 5 3 2 1 3 2 1

5 4 2 1 4 2 1 2 4 1 2 4 5

Broken Chord of C major

(b)

1 2 3 5 1 2 4 5 1 2 4 5 1 2 3 5 5 3 2 1 5 4 2 1 5 4 2 1 5 3 2 1

5 4 2 1 5 4 2 1 5 3 2 1 5 4 2 1 1 2 4 5 1 2 3 5 1 2 4 5 1 2 4 5

Arpeggios and broken chords

Arpeggio (It. = 'harp-like') means that the notes of a chord are played 'harp-wise' (i.e. in order, but one after the other), instead of being sounded together. The notes of a *broken chord* are similar to those of an *arpeggio*, but they are not in strict consecutive order. The *arpeggio* and broken chord of C major may be fingered as in Example 8.12.

In deciding the fingering of *arpeggios* and broken chords, all the notes of the chord should be considered together. The broken chord in Example 8.13 is fingered:

Example 8.13

The unbroken chord is fingered in the same way:

Example 8.14

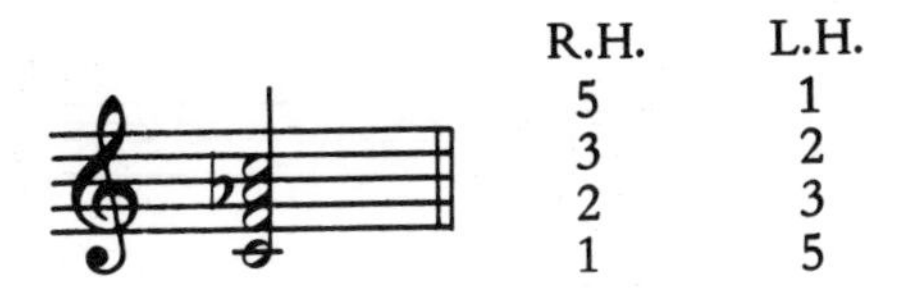

9

Theory of Piano Music (4)

Syncopation

Syncopation is, in general terms, the disturbance of normal rhythm, so that accents fall on beats, or parts of beats, which are not normally accented. The altered accent is often marked with a stress (>).

Example 9.1

Carnaval *Schumann Op. 9*

Notes of embellishment

These are ornamental notes (sometimes known as *grace notes*) which are placed before or after a principal note, and which are usually printed smaller than principal notes.

Ornamental notes were used by the early composers, chiefly to overcome the lack of sustaining power of the early keyboard instruments (spinet, virginals, harpsichord, etc.). The ornamentation of seventeenth- and eighteenth-century music is a specialised subject and is discussed in *The Interpretation of Music of the XVII and XVIII Centuries* (Arnold Dolmetsch), *The Interpretation of Early Music* (Robert Donington), and *Keyboard Interpretation*

(Howard Ferguson). Here we have space to note only the more usual methods of embellishment.

The *appoggiatura*, or 'leaning note', is a small note before the principal note, which takes half the value of the principal note if this is undotted, and two-thirds of its value if it is dotted.

Example 9.2

Written

Played

Written

Played

In modern music, composers give the *appoggiatura* its proper written value.

The *acciaccatura*, or 'crushing note', is written like the *appoggiatura*, but has a slanting stroke through the stem ♪. It is sounded on the beat, as quickly as possible before the principal note, which receives the accent.

Example 9.3

Written

Played

The *turn* (the sign ∾ placed over or after a note) consists of a figure of four notes (note above, note itself, note below, note itself). This figure is played either instead of, or after, the note itself.

Example 9.4

Written

Played

Written

Played

A sharp or flat, placed above or below the turn, means that the upper or lower note is to be sharpened or flattened.

Example 9.5

Played

The *inverted turn* (sign 𝆙 or 𝆘) is played in the same way as the turn, except that the figure consists of the note below, principal note, note above and note itself.

The *upper mordent* (sign 𝆝) consists of three notes (principal note, note above and principal note), played in rapid succession.

Example 9.6

Written

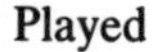

Played

The *lower mordent* (sign 𝆞) is played in the same way, except that the three notes consist of the principal note, note below and principal note.

The *trill*, or *shake* (sign *tr*~~) consists of the rapid alternation of the written note and the note above it; the trill usually ends with a turn.

Example 9.7

Written

tr~~~~

Played

In piano music a wavy or curved line is sometimes placed before a chord. A chord so marked is to be *spread*; i.e. the notes are to be played as an *arpeggio* in rapid succession from the lowest note upwards, each note being held as it is played – thus producing a harp-like effect.

Example 9.8

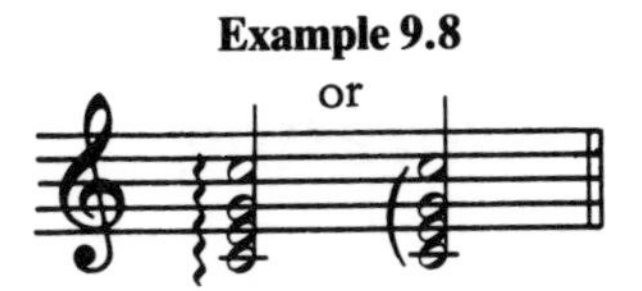

In a book of this size, it is impossible to describe the many rules of ornamentation which apply to music of different periods, particularly the baroque style of the seventeenth and eighteenth centuries. It may be said, however, that baroque trills and turns, with rare exceptions, begin on the upper note.

In well-edited editions of baroque and classical music, however, suggestions for the performance of ornaments are usually included as footnotes; these should, therefore, offer the necessary guidance to the pianist, until such time as enough experience has been gained to attempt a personal interpretation of these complex embellishments.

Self-testing questions

(Please see Preliminary remarks in Chapter 3, page 15.)

1 What is 'syncopation'? (*See page 74*)
2 What is an *appoggiatura*? How does it differ from an *acciaccatura*? (*See pages 75–6 and Examples 9.2 and 9.3*)
3 Write the sign for the 'turn'. Which notes does this figure consist of? (*See page 76, and Example 9.4*)
4 What is the effect of a sharp or flat, placed above or below a turn? (*See page 77, and Example 9.5*)
5 How does an 'inverted' turn differ from a normal one? (*See page 78*)
6 Of which notes does the *upper* mordent consist, and how are they played? Write the sign. (*See page 78, and Example 9.6*)
7 Of which notes does the *lower* mordent consist, and how are they played? Write the sign. (*See page 78*)
8 Write the sign for a trill or shake. Of which notes does it consist, and how does it usually end? (*See page 78, and Example 9.7*)
9 A wavy or curved line is sometimes placed before a chord, how should this chord be played? (*See page 79, and Example 9.8*)

10

Phrasing

Phrasing and Cadences

In verse and prose, punctuation marks (full stop, semi-colon, comma, etc.) are used to shape single words into sentences, clauses, and so on. Apart from serving as breathing spaces, their more important function is to provide 'thinking' places which will enable the reader to take in a number of words as a group, and so give proper meaning to a writer's thoughts. The other factor which gives shape to words is the accentuation of certain syllables, while other syllables are passed over more lightly.

Music also needs breathing and thinking places, and notes are therefore grouped into phrases and sentences by means of cadences.[1] These correspond to punctuation marks, and indicate points of repose – either complete or momentary. A phrase may consist of two or four bars, or sometimes of three, five, six or more bars. A musical 'sentence' may consist of two or more phrases.

Example 10.1 shows four different kinds of cadences.[2] If you play these cadences on the piano, you will find that (a) and (b) give the effect of complete repose, like the full stop, whereas (c) and (d) give the effect of a momentary pause without finality, like the comma or semi-colon. Although cadences appear in various forms,

[1] Cadence = a fall. In speech it is natural for the voice to fall at the end of a sentence. In music there is also often a falling off in flow and movement (but not necessarily in pitch) at a cadence.

[2] The *perfect cadence* is sometimes known as a *full close*; the *imperfect cadence* as a *half close*.

Example 10.1

(a) Perfect (or authentic) cadence
(b) Plagal cadence
(c) Imperfect cadence
(d) Interrupted (or deceptive) cadence

which it is not necessary at this stage to analyse individually, it is nevertheless important to be able to recognise points of complete or temporary repose, and to appreciate the feeling of progression towards the cadences. Without this feeling, music would be simply a succession of sounds, with no sense of continuity, of 'going somewhere'.

In Example 10.2, the arrows show the progression of each phrase towards its cadence, and when playing these bars this means thinking of phrases rather than beats or bars i.e. from the beginning to the end of each arrow. In addition, the progression from one phrase to another must be considered. In Example 10.2, although the cadence in the second bar may give the impression of a point of slight temporary repose, there must be no halt to the flow of the music. As soon, therefore, as you are able to play the notes with reasonable accuracy you should be thinking from the beginning of the music to the end of the fourth bar. In the second and fourth bars you will see that the chord at the end of each arrow is accentuated (*mfp*); this makes the shape of each phrase abundantly clear. (Note that *mfp* = *mezzo forte piano*: It. = half loud, half soft.)

Example 10.2

Sonata in G Minor — *Beethoven*
Op. 49, No. 1

Phrasing

In piano music notes may be played in different ways – smoothly, with one note connected to the next, or crisply, with each note separated. The smooth style of playing is known as *legato* (It. = smooth or connected) and the crisp style as *staccato* (It. = detached or separated). Curved lines, called *slurs*, are placed over or under groups of two or more notes of different pitch, showing that these groups should be played *legato*.

Example 10.3

The slur must not be confused with the *tie*, the short curved line which joins the third and fourth notes in Example 10.3. This is used to join together two or more notes of the *same* pitch, the first note being held down, and not sounded again.

Notes to be played *staccato* are indicated by dots placed over or under them. They are usually given approximately half their written value. Two other kinds of *staccato* are sometimes met with. Notes marked with a pointed dash (▾) are played *staccatissimo*, and held down for about a quarter of their full value. Notes marked with dots covered by a slur are played *mezzo-staccato* (or *semi-staccato*), and are held down for about three-quarters of their full value. In general, all notes not marked with *staccato* signs (even if not covered with slurs) are played *legato*, unless there is some general direction to the contrary, e.g. the word '*staccato*' may be used in place of dots.

Legato slurs *may* extend over entire phrases, but their duration does not necessarily coincide with that of phrases. In Example 10.2, for instance, each bar is slurred, whereas each phrase is actually two bars long. Slurs, therefore, are often used simply to indicate which notes are to be played smoothly and which are not. Just as, in verse or prose, it is not necessary to breathe at *every* comma, so in music we need not break the musical line at the end of every small group of sounds.

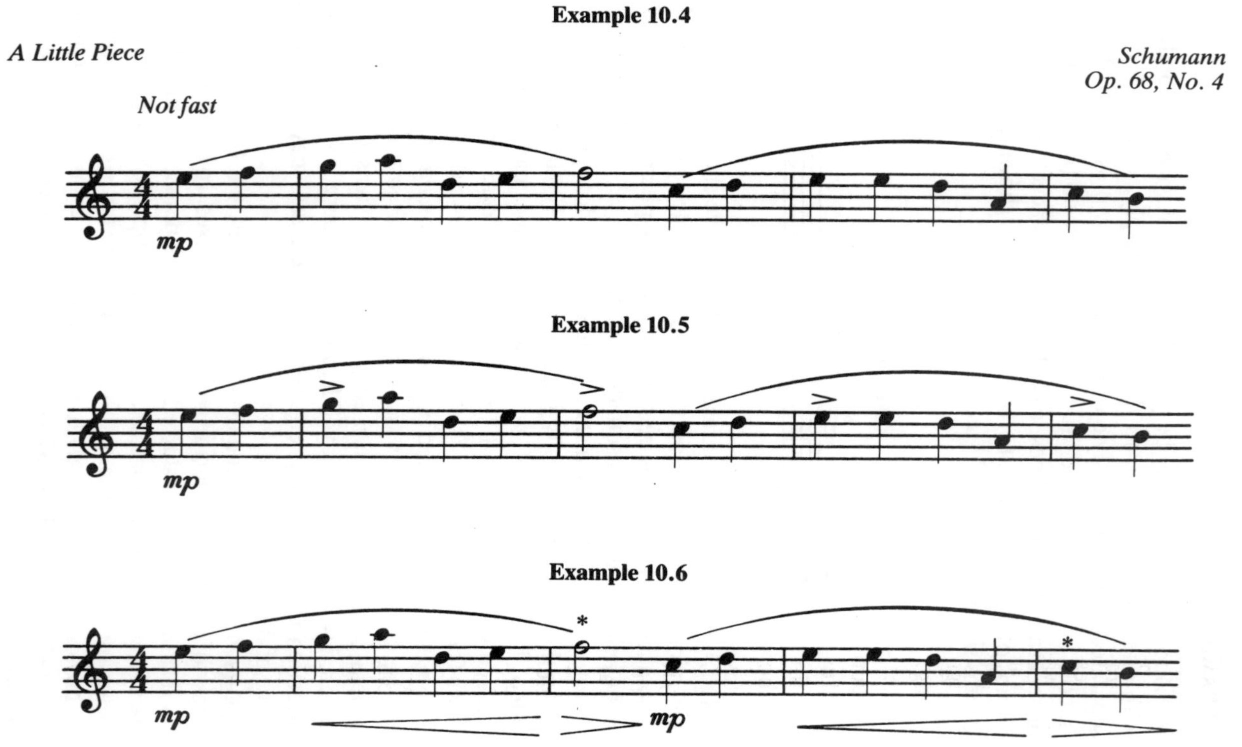
Example 10.4
A Little Piece
Schumann
Op. 68, No. 4
Not fast
mp
Example 10.5
mp
Example 10.6
*
mp
mp
*

As well as thinking from the beginning to the end of a phrase, it is important to appreciate its *shape*, so that you can interpret this in your playing. There is no better way of doing this than by thinking of a phrase as part of a song-melody, and singing it aloud during the process of practising (and *inwardly* when playing, or when you do not want to disturb people (e.g. on a bus). It is good practice to hum over simple melodies, such as folk, hymn or popular tunes, in which the progression of phrases is fairly obvious; this will make it easier to recognise the shape of more intricate phrases when they come along.

Let us now consider the first two phrases of a simple melody (Example 10.4).

Music theory tells us that in $\frac{4}{4}$ time the strongest accent falls on the first beat of each bar, so you *might* be tempted to play the melody as shown in Example 10.5.

However, if you sing the melody phrase by phrase, you will quickly realise that such a mechanical accentuation would completely destroy its shape and flow, and that something like Example 10.6 would be more appropriate. In this interpretation, the melody progresses towards the end of the phrases, and falls away on the notes marked with asterisks.

Here again, as well as thinking from the beginning of each phrase, your overall thinking needs to take in the flow from one phrase to the next, and thus cover both phrases. So we see that although there are accents on the first beat of each bar (except when a beat is displaced in syncopation), these accents may vary greatly in strength, and may sometimes be more apparent in the mind than in the music.

Phrasing in piano music is a complex art which ultimately depends on intuitive good sense and taste, but much can be learned by critical listening and study. In printed music, phrasing indicated by the composer or editor is not always satisfactory and care must be taken, perhaps with the help of an experienced pianist or piano dealer, to seek the best editions. In the early stages some general principles may be of help, provided they are not taken too literally.

When, for example, two notes of equal length are covered by a slur the first note is often stressed more than the second, which is made weaker and very slightly shorter, the finger being raised from the keyboard. A point which arises here is that a sound on the piano begins to fade as soon as it is heard. When two notes are slurred together, therefore, the sound of the first note will have faded a little by the time the second note is played (the slower the notes, the greater the fading). So the second note will need to be played a little more softly than the first, if it is to match. Careful listening and experiment are needed to achieve a perfect balance.

Example 10.7

Aria from Partita in G *Telemann*

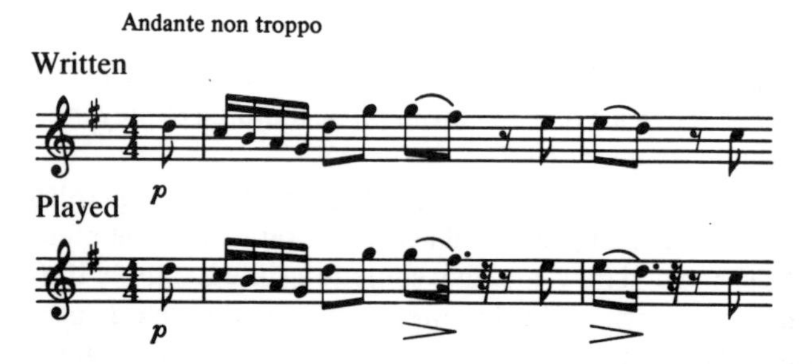

In larger groups of notes, the last note is sometimes shortened slightly by raising the hand from the keyboard, but this depends on the context of the melody. Singing a phrase quite naturally is usually the best way of deciding how it should be treated. Much may be learned by listening to records or tapes of fairly simple piano music and, at the same time, following the printed copy and carefully noting the style of phrasing, and the treatment of phrase and group endings. Suitable recorded pieces include:

Beethoven:	Sonata in G minor, Op 49, No 1
	Sonata in G major, Op 48, No 2
Bartók:	Ten Easy Pieces
	Nine Little Pieces
Schumann:	*Kinderscenen*, Op 15
Tchaikovsky:	Children's Album, Op 39

11

Tone Production

The piano keys

In order to throw a hammer against a string to make it sound, a piano key must be depressed fairly quickly. This requires a certain degree of muscular exertion of the finger – if there is too little, the hammer will merely be lifted, and there will be no sound. The quicker the key is depressed the louder will be the sound. A good sound is not produced, however, by striking the key, but rather by the exertion of the finger, and sometimes the weight of the arm. All tone, loud or soft, needs to be equally well controlled.

Once sound has been produced, it cannot be altered. If a key is held down (with the damper raised) the sound will continue, though it will gradually fade and eventually cease. It is therefore a waste of muscular energy to exert pressure on a key *after* the sound is heard, on the contrary, the finger muscles need to be relaxed at the moment the sound begins, so that the key is held down at its lowest point without pressure.

Arm movements

For tone production different parts of the arm are used for different purposes. A big, round tone may be obtained by using the whole arm from the shoulder, the weight of the arm and hand falling on the keys. To practise this, raise the arms and let them fall limply to the sides, like dead weights. Keeping the arms limp, raise them above the keyboard, and let them drop on to the keys; the fingers will fall naturally into a cup-like position.

When less tone is required (e.g. in slow *piano* and *mezzo-piano* chords), the weight of the forearm, moving from the elbow, may be used.

In more rapid technical passages, the hand may move from the wrist, or the keys may be depressed by the fingers alone. Arm weight may then be dispensed with, the arm being lightly held above the keyboard, with the forearm freely balanced and self-supporting, being neither tight nor relaxed.

Legato

In *legato* playing, one sound is carried over to the next without a break. The duration of a sound therefore depends upon when and how the piano keys are depressed and raised: this requires the most careful practice and listening. The speed at which the keys rise is controlled by the fingers, which do not leave the surface of the keys while they are rising. When moving from one key to another there is a slight rotary movement, as weight is transferred from one finger-tip to the next, rather like a see-saw. The attainment of a smooth *legato* depends on the critical judgement of both eye and ear. The fingers should be watched as weight passes from one finger to another, and the ear must confirm that there is neither a break between sounds, nor 'smudging' (caused by releasing one key *after* another has been put down). Both the beginning and the end of a sound must be listened to.

A true *legato*, such as is possible on the violin, is impossible on the piano because of the nature of the instrument. The pianist's task is therefore to create the illusion of *legato*, often with the help of the damper pedal. Also, because of the percussive character of the piano, a succession of notes played with precisely equal strength often fails to give the impression of *legato* playing. Hence the importance of gradations of tonal strength – rises and falls (*crescendo* and *diminuendo*) in musical phrases. In the early stages such gradations, if used at all, are often exaggerated. Subtlety is only acquired by observation, experience, and the development of the 'inner ear'.

Staccato

Staccato notes are short, and separated from each other by a brief period of silence. *Staccato* playing is made possible by the action of the piano dampers which, by falling back on the strings as soon as the keys are released, bring the sound to an end. True *staccato* is short and crisp, but in deciding the exact duration of *staccato* notes, the style, mood and speed of the music must be taken into account. In Example 11.1, the notes are given half their written value.

Example 11.1

Staccatissimo notes (sometimes marked with dashes) may be given approximately a quarter of their written value.

Example 11.2

Allegretto

Written

Played

Mezzo-staccato notes may be given approximately three-quarters of their written value.

Example 11.3

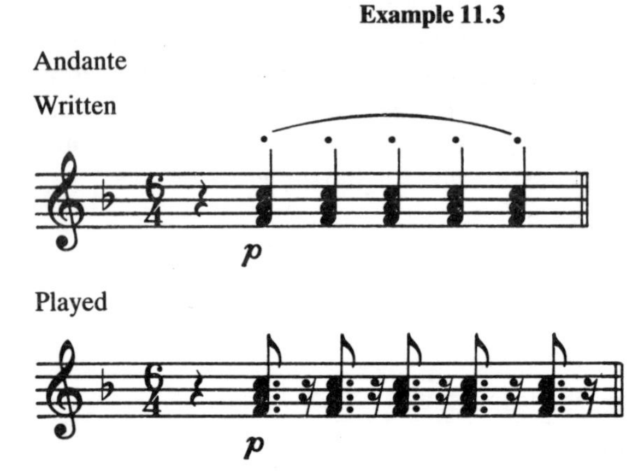

Staccato notes may be played: with the fingers, which are withdrawn from the keys without waiting for them to rise; with the wrist, which also rebounds rapidly from the keys; with the forearm, the wrist being firm and not allowed to droop; or with the whole arm. The method used depends on the context of the music. In general, finger action may be effective for quick, crisp *staccato*, wrist action for light chords and octaves, forearm action for heavier effects, and whole arm action for *bravura* ('brilliant') passages.

Finger position

For brilliant passage work (scales, *arpeggios* and so on), the fingers should be well curved, otherwise it will not be possible to depress the keys clearly and incisively. The fingers should also be curved when full tone is needed in chord passages, etc.

In *cantabile* (singing) passages, however, an almost flat finger action is often used, the fingers seeming to cling to the keys.

Before trying to produce *any* kind of tone, the appropriate 'tone-colour' should be imagined, so that the mental image can be compared with the actual sound.

Forearm rotation

In piano playing, some kind of rotary action is required almost continually. It is not possible to rotate the hand from the wrist, so that rotary action must come from the forearm and shoulder. In broken octaves the rotary action is most pronounced.

Example 11.4

With smaller intervals, the rotary movement is less obvious, or scarcely perceptible. In forearm rotation, the muscular energy with which a key is depressed must be relaxed as soon as the sound is heard, and transferred to the next key, and so on, backwards and forwards from one key to another. The rotary movement should not be exaggerated though, and the fingers should not be raised higher than necessary. During this movement the hand should be kept on a level with the forearm; there should be sufficient tension at the wrist to ensure this.

12

The Pedals

The damper pedal

In piano music it is customary to use the sign 'Ped' when the damper pedal is to be depressed, and the sign * when it is to be released; alternatively, the duration of the pedalling may be shown by the sign └───┘. These markings are not always to be relied on, and a good deal of music has either no pedal markings, or simply a general 'con ped' (with pedal). Although, as a beginner, you will have to rely on pedal markings in the best edited editions you can find, it is important that you should learn to decide for yourself when and how to use the pedal.

The damper pedal has been called the 'soul' of the piano, and when used in a sensitive way it can impart glowing effects of colour to imaginative music, and make possible *legato* passages which could not be played by the hands alone. But it is no easy matter to decide exactly when, and how, the damper pedal should be used; indeed there is often a difference of opinion among experts. (To what extent, for example, should the pedal be used in Bach's keyboard music?) In the early stages you are advised to err on the side of caution, and to start by using very little pedal indeed. Then, as experience is gained, you can gradually add to your pedal technique.

By lifting the dampers from the strings the damper pedal sustains the sound, and also enriches it by setting other strings free to vibrate in sympathy. If, however, the pedal is thoughtlessly used, clarity of phrasing and sound may be sacrificed, and playing which would otherwise be good, spoiled. Let us take a simple example.

Example 12.1

Remembrance (Album for the Young) *Schumann*
Op. 68, No. 28

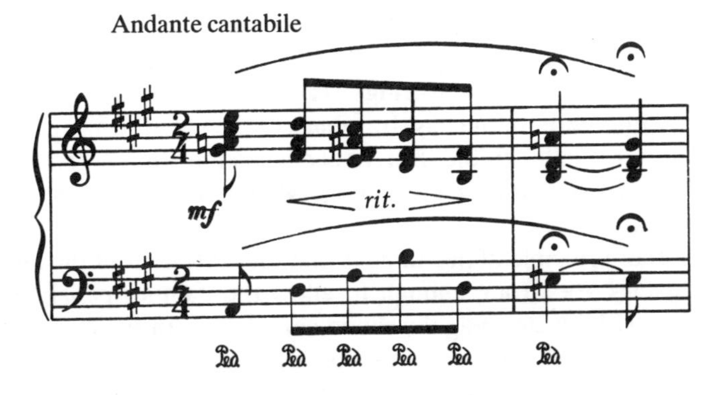

In Example 12.1, if the damper pedal were to be held down throughout the passage, the result would be a meaningless jumble of sounds. Try it and see. It follows, therefore, that the pedal should normally be changed each time there is a change of harmony. If each chord is separately pedalled, as indicated, the passage may indeed be enriched. But how is the pedalling to be done? The normal inclination would be to move the hands and the foot together, depressing the pedal at the precise moment that each chord is played. But a succession of *different* chords can be bound together more smoothly if what is known as 'syncopated pedalling' is used. To practise this, depress the pedal *after* you have played a chord, lift it at the precise moment that you play the next chord, and then depress it again. Syncopated pedalling is by far the most common form, and as a general rule the foot should move after the hand. The time lapse between one movement and the other needs to be very nicely judged. For example, the upper strings of the piano vibrate more quickly than the lower ones, so when playing high chords it may be possible to depress the pedal almost immediately it is raised, but when low bass notes are played (especially if *forte*) more time may have to be allowed for the change of pedal, so that the strings can be completely dampened. The exact duration may vary from piano to piano, so that very sensitive listening and careful experiment is needed to ensure that there is no blurring of consecutive sounds.

Occasionally, the damper pedal may be used 'on the beat' (i.e. simultaneously with the hands) for short, isolated chords, for example.

The top strings of the piano, having no dampers, are not affected by the pedal, and those upper strings which do have dampers are less affected than the lower strings. It is therefore possible to sustain one or more notes in the bass by means of the pedal, while playing light passages in the treble. But, as in all pedalling, it is necessary to try this effect so that the ear can judge whether or not the result will be blurred.

Another principle of pedalling is that the vibrations of the heavy bass strings are strong enough to allow the damper pedal to be changed without stopping the sound completely. In Example 12.2, for instance, the left hand cannot hold down the bass octave, and at the same time play the soft moving chords. If the pedal is held down throughout the bar, it may be found that the last two chords are blurred when the harmony changes. To avoid this, the pedal could be put down as soon as the bass octave is played. Then, after each of the last two chords, the pedal could be lifted and depressed as quickly as possible, the dampers would not have time to check the vibrations completely, so that the bass octave would continue to sound throughout the bar. This technique is known as 'half-pedalling'.

Example 12.2

Although there are exceptions to every rule, broadly speaking the damper pedal should not be used in *staccato* passages, or where there are very rapid changes of harmony. It is important that the pedal should be used only for a specific purpose – never to cover up clumsy fingering or inadequate technique. This is why it is usually best to practise for some little time without the pedal, adding it only when a satisfactory degree of accuracy is evident to the ear. When progress has been made in elementary control of the pedal more detailed information may be sought from books such as *Points of Pedalling*, by James Ching (Forsyth), or *Pedalling the Modern Pianoforte* (Oxford University Press).

The left pedal

The use of the left pedal weakens the sound of the strings, producing tone-colour of a veiled or muted quality. The pedal should not be used merely to produce a soft tone which must be obtained from the fingers. The use of the soft pedal is indicated by the words *una corda* (It. = one string) for depression, and *tre corde* (three strings) for release. Sometimes the left pedal and damper pedal are used together.

13

Technique and Interpretation

Scales

Scales and *arpeggios* are the basis of many piano passages, as a glance at almost any piece of piano music will show. Regular practice of scales and *arpeggios* is therefore a major source of the pianist's technical equipment, leading to fluency and agility, and also to control of different tone qualities.

To make scales more interesting they can be played at different speeds, with different gradations of tone, and with different rhythms such as the following:

Example 13.1

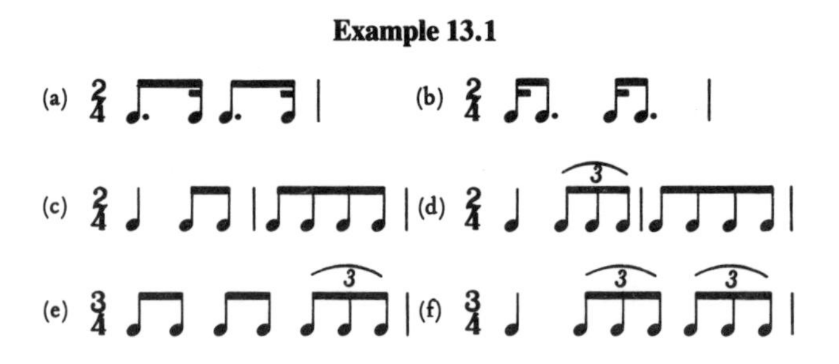

Scales may be played in two octaves or sometimes, for a change, in three or four. The pattern of fingering should be always be studied from the scale book before a new scale is attempted, and this pattern should then be memorised. Each hand should be practised separately, and only when each is reasonably perfect should a scale be played with both hands together.

Example 13.2

Exercises to facilitate passing the thumb under the finger, and the finger over the thumb (repeat each section several times)

Right Hand

Left Hand

Demonstration Lesson Two should be studied in conjunction with this chapter, and the exercises in Example 13.2 should also be practised.

These exercises are in the key of C, but they can be transposed into other keys, using your scale book if necessary. *Freedom Technique* (Oxford University Press) contains many useful, short exercises which are of help when practising scales, *arpeggios*, etc.

Arpeggios and broken chords

The technical difference between broken chords and *arpeggios* is that whereas, in both forms, the hand is shifted up or down the keyboard, in *arpeggios* the thumb is also passed under the fingers, and the fingers over the thumb (the fingering of each form is shown in Example 8.12). The passing under of the thumb needs to be watched very carefully, and *arpeggios* should be played quite slowly at first, one hand at a time. The wrist and arm must be free, and the wrist raised as soon as the thumb passes under the fingers. The elbow should not be allowed to jerk upwards or outwards when the thumb passes under, but should be adjusted as quietly as possible to the new position.

The exercises in Example 13.3 will help to develop the smooth passage of the thumb and fingers.

Example 13.3

Arpeggio of C Major
(repeat several times)

Right Hand

Left Hand

2 1 4 4 1 2

3 3

Unevenness in *arpeggio* playing may be helped by accenting different notes in turn (Example 13.4).

Example 13.4

Skips and leaps

Large skips between notes are often difficult to judge accurately, but they may not appear as large as they look if you think of the first note as a kind of pivot upon which you can swing round towards the second note (the fingers should be over the keys before putting them down). If you are playing a succession of similar skips (octaves, for example, with the thumb and little finger), keep the hand extended so that the distance between the fingers remains the same for each skip.

In leaping to chords from a distance (for example, in the left hand part of a waltz) the feeling again should be of getting over the notes before playing them. Sometimes, with a four- or five-note chord, it is helpful to practise leaping first to the middle notes of the chord before playing it complete. When playing skips and leaps the hand should normally be kept as close to the keys as possible. Awkward passages should be memorised, and practised first with open, then with closed, eyes. When leaping, the arm should be moved from the shoulder. The distance of the 'jump' can be measured by placing the elbow over the first note or chord, and moving it to the second. A good exercise is to prepare the hand for a chord while keeping it above the keys, then to play the chord and repeat it (in other octaves) all over the piano.

Trills

Trills are difficult to play, and should be practised quite slowly and softly, the fingers remaining on the surface of the keys with the muscles relaxed. Any inequality of tone between one finger and another may then be heard and corrected. The comparative weakness of the fourth and little fingers will need to be allowed for when they are used. Notes which are evenly matched in tone and completely regular should be sought. A slow trill, really well played, is better than a fast one which is uneven.

Chords

Chord playing, so far as loudness or softness is concerned, depends on the speed with which piano keys are depressed. For brilliant, heavy chords the keys are moved suddenly downwards, using arm weight from the shoulders. For soft chords the keys are moved more slowly downwards, using forearm weight from the elbows. In chord-playing it is essential that all the notes of a chord should be put down precisely together. 'Ragged' chords are more likely to be heard in very soft music, since it is not always easy to depress several keys together when they are put down slowly.

With *staccato* chords the hand should be allowed to rise with the keys as soon as the sound is heard or has reached the desired length (see Chapter 10, page 83). The hand should not be snatched up, however. Unless the fingers are required to play other notes, they may remain on the surface of the keys.

With *legato* chords only the fingers (not the weight of the arm) should be used to hold down the keys once the sound has been heard.

Interpretation

We can barely scratch the surface of this subject, which needs a book to itself.[1] Interpretation implies an intelligent, commonsense approach to the performance of a piece of music. But intelligence and common sense are personal attributes, and so far as interpretation of music is concerned there is bound to be a wide divergence of opinion. Indeed, without it, music would be dull, as would *Hamlet* if every actor played the title role in the same way. There are, however, certain general principles which are usually accepted, and

[1] *Interpretation in Piano Study* by Joan Last (Oxford University Press) is an excellent book for the serious piano student; as also is her *Freedom in Piano Technique*.

in the Demonstration Lessons some of these have been applied to elementary situations.

Interpretation is, in effect, a creative (or re-creative) element in the performance of music, in which the performer attempts to interpret a piece of music according to his own judgement and personality. Judgement is the outcome of an observation and experience, and in the early stages we must be content to progress very slowly, and to lean heavily on the opinions of performers whose talent and experience we have come to respect.

Nevertheless, it may be useful to discuss some basic matters of interpretation. In studying piano music we should take into account the nature of the music, the composer, and the period during which it was written. We can then decide on the style of playing which would be appropriate. This may lead us to further research to find out how the music was performed at the time it was written. With the early composers – Scarlatti and Bach, for example – this will not be easy, and there may be no conclusive results. But it is always worthwhile, and invariably fascinating, to find out as much as possible about a composer and the times in which he lived. Biographies, programmes on radio and television, records and tapes, reviews and articles in journals and newspapers, all may contribute to the general picture.

It is also important to take note of the 'plan' of a piece, to appreciate the phrasing, chord structure, cadences, and so on, and to realise where the music is 'going'. Most pieces build up to climaxes at certain points, and you should look for these. If a passage is to be increased in intensity towards the climax, the approach should be carefully thought out. A *crescendo* must not be begun too soon or too loudly, or its power will be exhausted before the climax is reached. Similarly, a *decrescendo* must be made gradually.

A phrase may also have a climax – perhaps at the highest, lowest, loudest or softest note. In Example 13.5, for instance, the climax (marked with an *) occurs on the second beat of the second bar.

The study of musical 'forms', which is of considerable importance to the advanced pianist, cannot be entered into in a book of this size. *The Form of Music* by William Cole (Associated Board) is of practical help to the serious student.

Example 13.5

Träumerei (Kinderscenen) | *Schumann*
Op. 15, No. 7

Accompaniment and melody

If a melody is played on a violin, accompanied by a piano, the difference in the tone quality of the two instruments will make it easy for the listener to distinguish between the melody and the accompaniment. On the piano, however, there is one basic tone-quality, so that the difference can only be made clear by playing the accompaniment more softly than the melody. Sometimes both melody and accompaniment are played by the same hand; the weight of the arm must then be concentrated on those fingers which are playing the melody, and the accompaniment must be played more lightly with the other fingers.

In Example 13.6 the accompaniment is played by the right hand, and the melody alternately by the left and right hands. In order to play this perfectly smoothly, the tone of the left hand must be matched exactly with that of the right hand.

Rubato

Rubato might well be described as 'robbing Peter to pay Paul'. If, in music of an expressive character, every note of a melody is played with mathematical precision, the result will be dull and mechanical rather than expressive. The pianist will therefore sometimes linger over a certain note or phrase in the interest of more intense

Example 13.6

Liebesträume *Liszt*

expression. When some notes are minutely lengthened, other notes in the same bar or phrase may be minutely shortened, so that the entire bar or phrase remains the same length as if it had been played strictly in time. These minute variations are too subtle to be expressed in musical notation: they are spontaneous rather than planned, and vary according to the artistic feeling of the performer. The effective use of *rubato* requires a wealth of experience and maturity of judgement. Excessive or exaggerated use can too easily lead to major abuse, but much can be learned by careful listening to the playing of great artists while following the music.

Accents and pauses

Accents can be performed in many different ways, and exactly what is appropriate to a particular note or chord can only be decided after studying the context of the music. Clearly an accent will be less heavy in a soft passage than in a loud one. There will also be a difference between an accented *legato* note and an accented *staccato* one. Generally, a *legato* accent will have more depth, and a *staccato* accent more percussive attack.

A pause over a note shows that it is to be sustained for longer than its normal value. Again the exact length can only be judged in the context of the music which precedes and follows the pause. A pause mark may also be placed over a rest, when this is to be made longer than usual. A pause sign placed over a bar-line indicates a short silence, also, the sign is sometimes placed over the final double-bar, to denote the end of a composition.

Phrase endings

In performance, 'breathing' places between phrases (see page 80) are often indicated by very slight breaks in the musical sound, even when there is no break in the printed music (i.e. when the final note of a phrase is not followed by a rest). In Example 10.6, for instance, the last note of each of the two phrases can be minutely shortened. It is important, however, that such tiny breaks should be subtly 'tailored', according to the character of the music (often they will be 'felt' rather than heard). They must not cause the continuity and 'flow' of the music to be disturbed.

14

Tension and Relaxation

The basis of modern piano technique is the proper use of tension and relaxation of the muscles used in piano playing, as well as the application of arm weight (originating at the shoulder), rotary freedom, and so on. Tobias Matthay (1858–1945), the English pianist and teacher, was one of the first to stress the importance of muscular relaxation.

Tension is often used synonymously with stress to describe a condition of emotional anxiety, and this of course may affect the performance of the pianist, though a degree of emotional tension is a necessary contribution to the intensity of the performance.

Physical tension, however, is concerned with muscular exertion, and without some degree of this kind of tension we should not be capable of any human activity, let alone playing the piano. Physical tension can be necessary or unnecessary, sufficient or excessive. So while we need tension to depress a piano key, we may find that our finger action is inhibited by simultaneous unnecessary tension in other parts of the body. Also, when we have just depressed a piano key, we must learn to control the tension, so that the key is held down without further pressure until such time as we want it to rise. This means that tension must be reduced as soon as the sound is heard.

Although most pianists might benefit from short, regular periods of total relaxation, if you became totally relaxed at the piano the chances are that you would fall off the piano stool! So we need to use 'differential' relaxation, in which unnecessary tension is eliminated so far as is possible, although it is probable that *some* degree of 'residual' tension is always present. Thus, when we are using our fingers we must try to avoid stiffness in other parts of the body, and so on. In short, the more we learn to recognise feelings of tension and relaxation, the more we may hope to bring them under our control.

Differential relaxation may be practised when lying down or sitting in a chair and moving the fingers as in piano playing, while keeping the rest of the body relaxed. Then, still moving the fingers, (a) raise the wrists, (b) raise the elbows, and (c) raise the arms from the shoulders. Differential relaxation, if regularly and correctly practised, will help to reduce many unnecessary tensions, and to produce muscular harmony between the different parts of the body.

Tension and relaxation and the pianist

Deep, easy breathing is extremely important for the pianist. There are times when the breathing has to be matched to the length of a phrase, so that it is not rushed at the end because of shortness of breath. Breathing does, in fact, have a profound effect on the whole nervous system; a few deep breaths will often help to re-establish control over a situation which has become difficult because of some kind of mental anxiety. Because gentle exhalation helps to release unnecessary tension, it is logical to start a piece or scale while breathing out, rather than while breathing in. Try it both ways, and decide for yourself.

If, when practising, you become aware of undue tension or stiffness in any part of the body, stop and relax the muscles. Tense the hands, for instance, and then let go completely, or flex the forearm and let go, or stand with arms falling limply to sides, chin on chest and shoulders flopping forward, like a rag doll.

A useful exercise at the piano is to make small semi-circular movements with the entire arms, from the shoulders to the tips of the fingers. Each movement starts with both thumbs on Middle C, and then travels to the Cs two octaves above and below Middle C, played with the little fingers. This movement, repeated several times slowly and gently, will help to eliminate stiffness, and to introduce a feeling of relaxation.

When practising quick passages such as scales, it is useful to begin by playing each note slowly, quickly moving the finger into the key, then relaxing as much pressure as possible as soon as the sound is heard before moving to the next note.

Another useful exercise to free the wrist of unnecessary tension is to play a chord softly, say:

Example 14.1

Then move the wrist gently and slowly up and down, keeping the fingers lightly on the keys, and making sure that the hand is free from stiffness.

Since all parts of the body are interdependent, stiffness or unnecessary tension in one part is likely to affect another. If, for example, the fingers of the right hand are stiff when playing, the fingers of the left hand may also be stiff, *even when not playing*. A faulty position of one part of the body will therefore have to be dealt with before stiffness in another part of the body can be eliminated. The Alexander Technique, which is taught at many music colleges, is based on the theory that the correct relationship between the head, neck and back can free the whole body from harmful tension. The technique can be learned from a qualified teacher, but quite a long period of study is required.

The ideal in piano playing is to play as well as possible with the least possible effort, but no firm recommendations can be offered to achieve this happy state of affairs. Habits such as raising the shoulders unduly, or hunching them, may cause tensions and wasted effort and should be avoided: but many eminent pianists exhibit similar 'failings'. The most you can do is to take note of your general attitude and playing position, and to try to modify this when you become aware of unnecessary tension or stiffness. Irritating habits however, should be eliminated as soon as possible – foot-tapping, head-wagging, grimacing, etc. Habits resulting from nervousness or excitement (even when practising alone) may be treated by general relaxation away from the piano, and by careful attention to breathing.

For those with special problems, such as the adult beginner with stiff or arthritic fingers, tensing and relaxing the hands between playing may be particularly beneficial. Although, in general, piano playing should help to prevent arthritic fingers from becoming more stiff, care should always be taken to avoid excessive practice, since pain in any part of the body may cause undue tension.

15

Improvisation

Improvisation is music which is created as it is performed, without previous preparation or detailed notation. Improvisation was once considered of great importance, and was a skill much practised by keyboard performers such as Bach, Mozart and Beethoven; in 1747, for example, Bach improvised a fugue on a theme devised by Frederick the Great, which he subsequently developed in his *Musical Offering*. In modern times, jazz musicians have improvised melodies against a harmonic, or modal, background, and improvised passages have appeared in 'aleatory' music, which contains elements of chance, or random selection. Nowadays, improvisation may be applied to a wide variety of skills, ranging from elaborate extemporisations by organists or other keyboard performers, which may involve a high degree of compositional talent, to the reproduction, or harmonisation, of existing music.

Some people have a natural gift for 'playing by ear' music which they have heard, sometimes with a remarkable degree of accuracy. Those who do not possess this gift may, with practice, acquire sufficient skill to enable them to harmonise melodies, and possibly to attempt simple composition, at the piano. To attain this skill, some knowledge of harmonic progression is necessary.

Triads

On page 46 we have seen that triads may be formed on each note of the major and minor scale. The three most important triads are those formed on the first, fourth and fifth degrees of the major or minor scale (Example 15.1).

Example 15.1

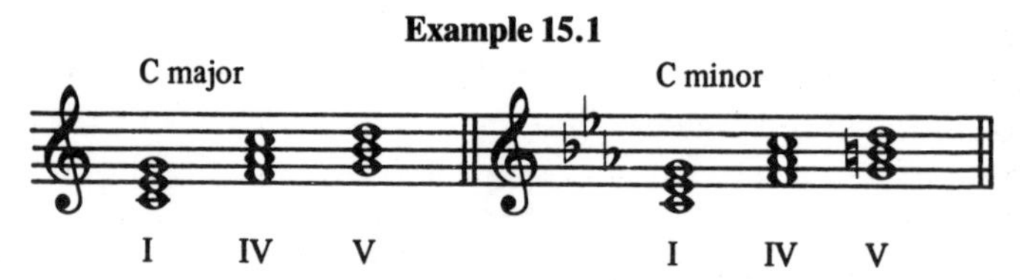

These three triads are called *primary triads*, whereas the remaining triads are known as *secondary triads*. In Example 15.1, in which the *root* (fundamental note from which the chord originates) is the lowest note of the chord, the triads are said to be in *root position*. These triads may be in *close harmony* (in which the notes of the chords are kept close together), or in *open harmony* (with gaps between one or more of the upper notes), and any of the three notes may be the highest note.

Example 15.2

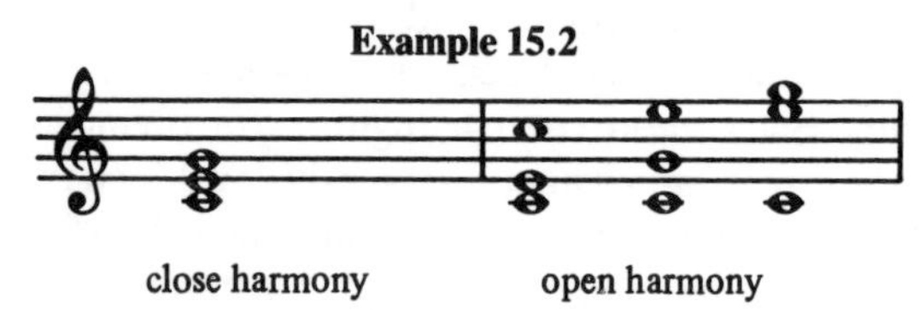

When harmony is in more than three parts, one or more notes of the triad must be doubled, either at the unison, i.e. the combined sound of two notes at the same pitch (Example 15.3) or at the octave (Example 15.4).

Example 15.3

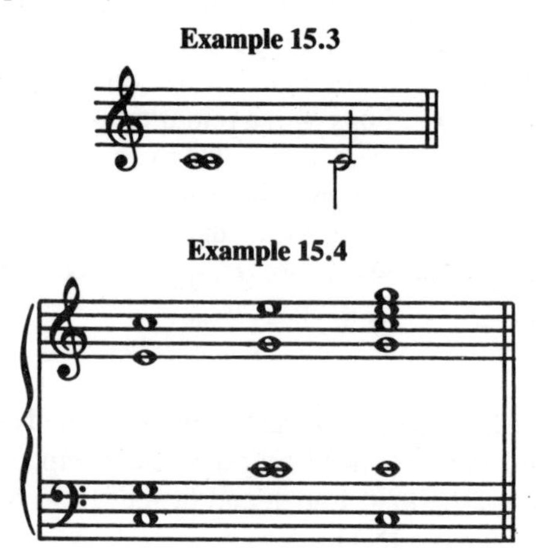

Example 15.4

Inverted triads

The notes of a triad may be arranged so that one of the upper notes becomes the lowest; the triad is then said to be *inverted*. Example 15.5 shows the tonic triad of C major in (a) root position with the root as the lowest note, (b) first inversion with the third as the lowest note, and (c) second inversion with the fifth as the lowest note. The chords are usually figured I, Ib, Ic.

Example 15.5

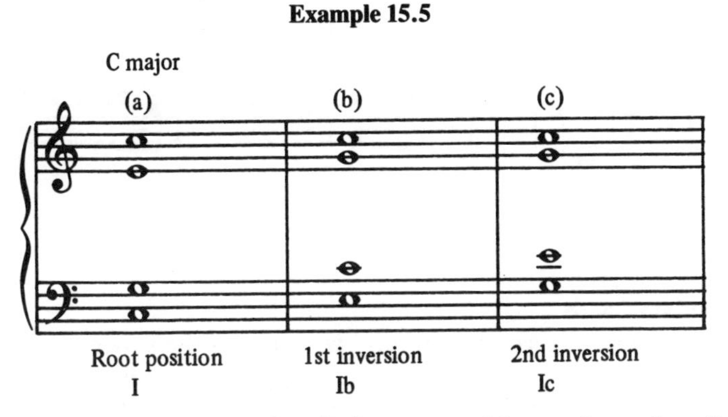

With the three primary chords, in root position or inversion, it is possible to harmonise simple melodies.

Example 15.6

Baa, Baa, Black Sheep

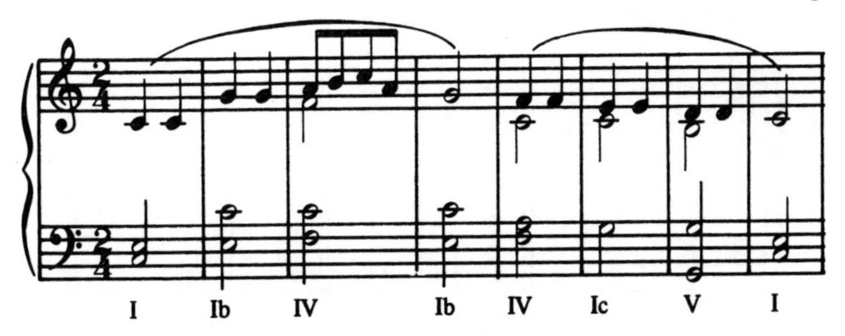

In the third bar of Example 15.6, the second quaver is treated as a *passing note*, i.e. a melody note taken scalewise between two notes which are part of the harmony, and which does not require separate harmonisation.

A more florid accompaniment might be effected by using broken chords in the left hand, on these lines:

Example 15.7

Secondary triads

The most useful secondary triads are those on the supertonic and the submediant. In major keys the supertonic triad is minor (see page 47), and may be used in either root position or first inversion. In minor keys it is diminished, and is better in first inversion. The most useful progression is from the supertonic to the dominant.

Example 15.8

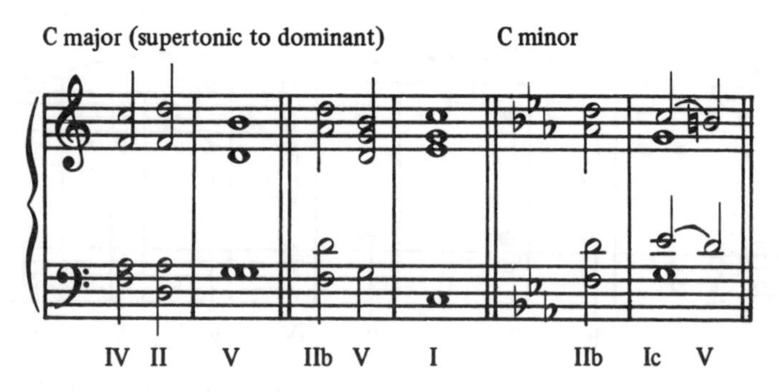

The submediant triad is mostly used in root position, and is often preceded by the dominant triad, to form an interrupted cadence (see page 81).

Example 15.9

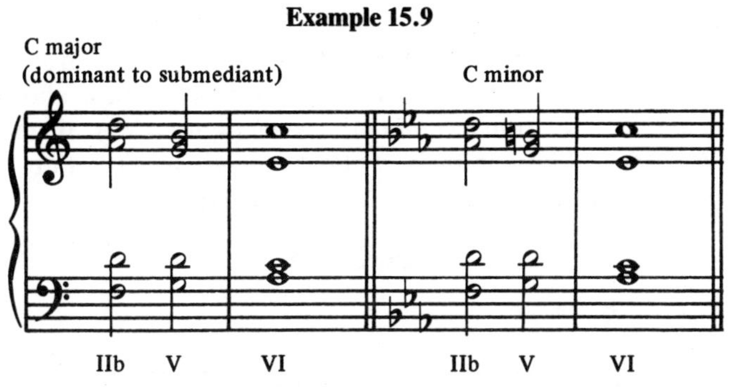

Using these secondary chords we could play:

Example 15.10

The last two bars form a plagal cadence (see page 81). In more florid style, we could play:

Example 15.11

Dominant sevenths

If we add a note to a triad, a seventh above the root, we form a *chord of the seventh*. If the added note is a minor seventh above a dominant root, we form a *dominant seventh* (figured V7). Since this consists of four different notes, it may be used in root position, and in three inversions (figured V7b, V7c and V7D).

Example 15.12

In root position, the dominant seventh may be used instead of the dominant triad. The inversions may be used freely, and are often effective as a half beat between two notes which are a third apart (as at (a) in Example 15.13).

Example 15.13

Other chords

When a fourth note is added to a major or minor triad, a major or minor seventh above the root, a chord is formed which is useful, in root position, to harmonise a melody which moves up the scale.

Example 15.14

Triads with 7ths added above the root

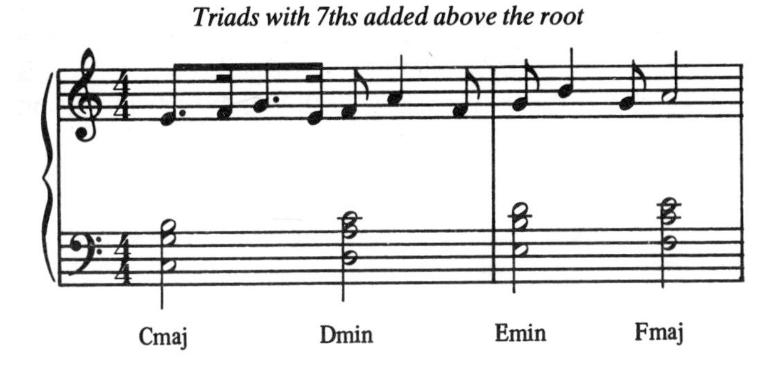

When a note a major sixth above the root is added to a major or minor triad, the following chord is produced.

Example 15.15

Triad with major 6th added above the root

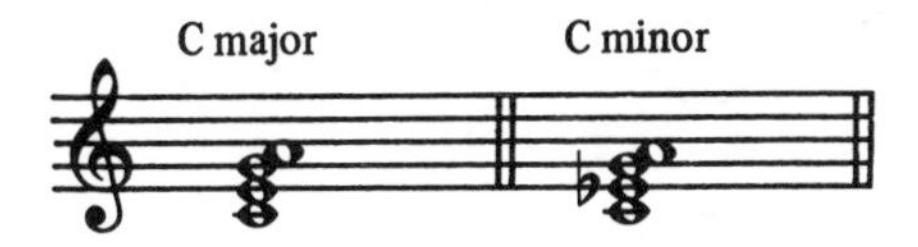

This can often produce a more interesting accompaniment than that provided by the triad.

Example 15.16.

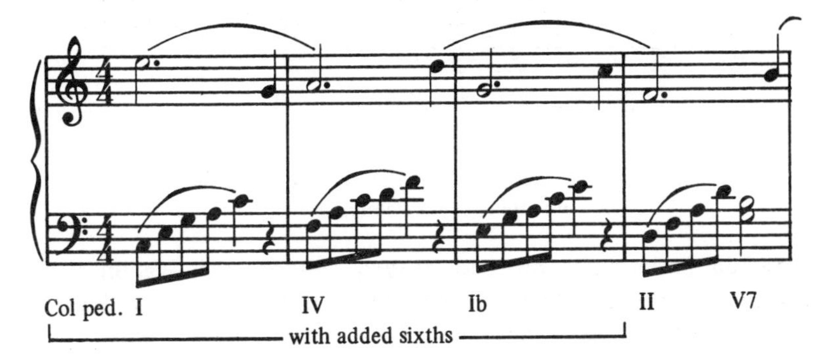

Modulation

Music which constantly remains in the same key often lacks melodic interest and variety of harmonisation; except for some short melodies, therefore, music tends to pass from one key to another and back again. When the new key is firmly established the music is said to *modulate* to that key, and this modulation is often effected by using a *pivot chord* (i.e. a chord common to both the old key and the new one), followed by a *modulating chord* which is usually the dominant seventh of the new key.

Example 15.17

(a) *pivot chord* (VI in C major = II in G major) (b) modulating chord (V7 in G major) * = passing notes

Modulation may also proceed through a chord which has one or more notes belonging to both the old and the new keys; these are known as *pivot notes*.

Example 15.18

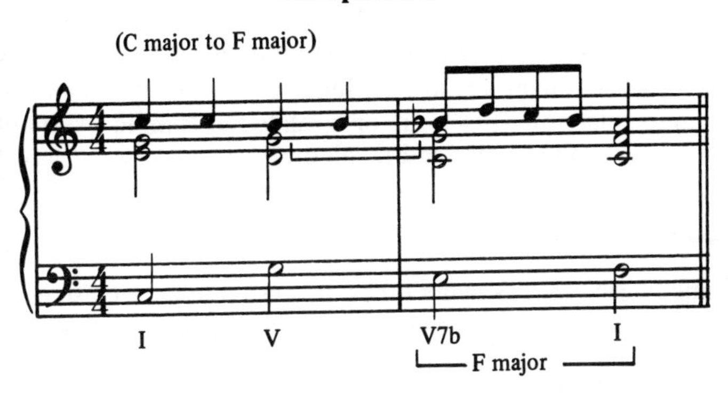

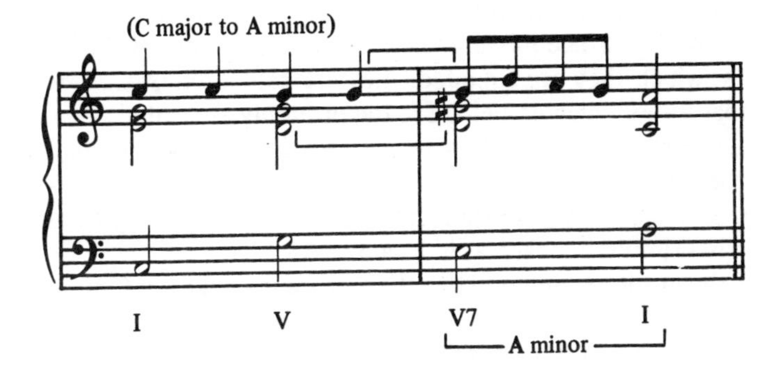

(C major to E minor)

I V V7c I

E minor

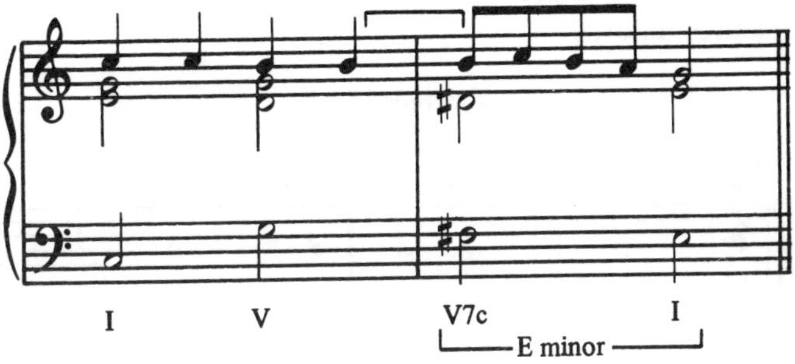

⌴ = *pivot note*

Modulation from one key to any other key is possible, but the most simple and natural modulation is when music passes from one key to another key to which it is closely related (i.e. the relative minor (or major), the dominant key and its relative, and the sub-dominant key and its relative). Thus C major is related to A minor, G major and E minor, and F major and D minor.

Melodic decoration

In some music, such as hymn tunes, it is usual to harmonise every note of a melody, but in piano and other music this is seldom necessary or desirable, and more often melody notes move up and down the scale, above a single sustained chord (or broken chord).

We have already mentioned the passing note in the third bar of Example 15.6. Since passing notes do not form part of the chord against which they are sounded, they are called *unessential notes*, whereas notes which do belong to the harmony are called *essential*. Thus, in Example 15.14, the second note of the melody is a passing (unessential) note, whereas all the other melody notes belong to the harmony, and are therefore essential. Passing notes may occur in two parts simultaneously, as in Example 15.17.

All the music examples in this chapter are in the key of C major or minor, and they should be *transposed* (i.e. played at another pitch, and therefore in a different key) into as many keys as possible, so that the harmonic progression becomes familiar. For example, the first four bars of Example 15.6 could be transposed into the keys of B flat and F major.

Example 15.19

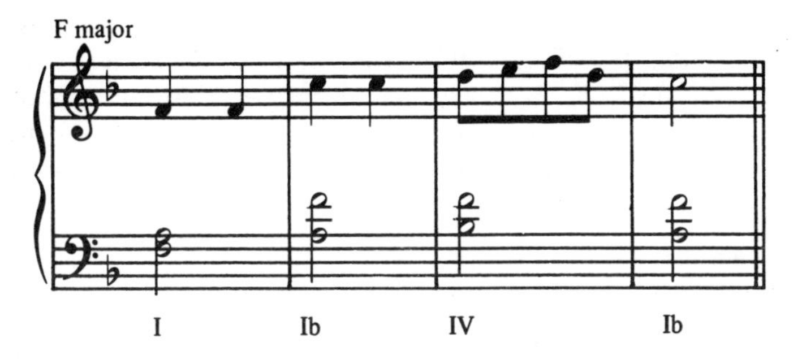

Style

Finally, different styles of accompaniment must be considered. In improvising an accompaniment to a melody (existing or invented), the style of the music must be taken into account. As an exercise, let us develop this basic melody in various styles.

Example 15.20

1 As a *march*:

Example 15.21

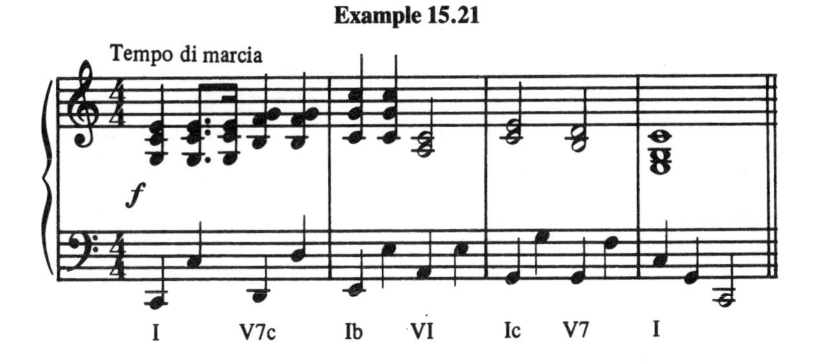

2 As a *waltz*:

Example 15.22

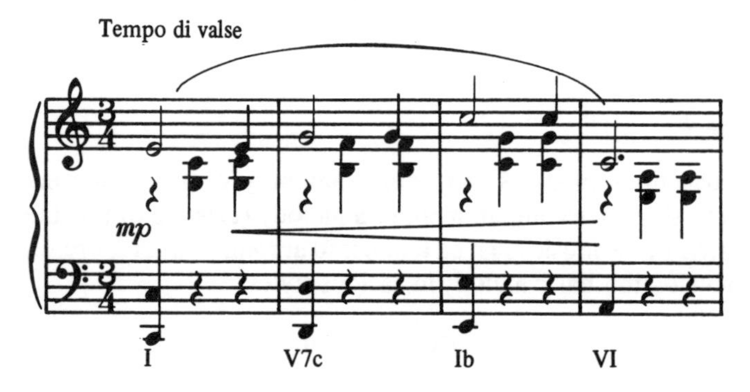

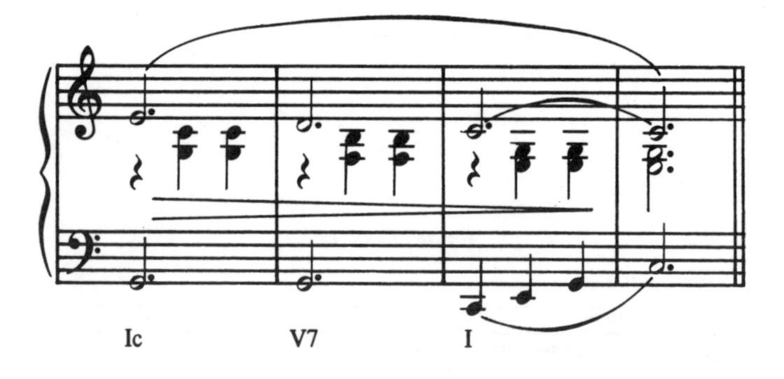

3 As a *lullaby*:

Example 15.23

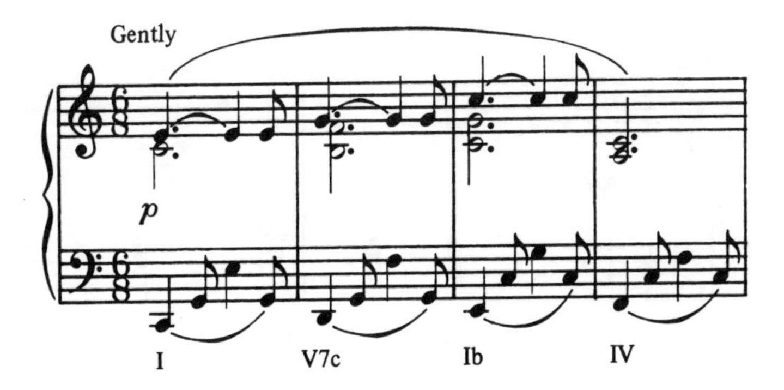

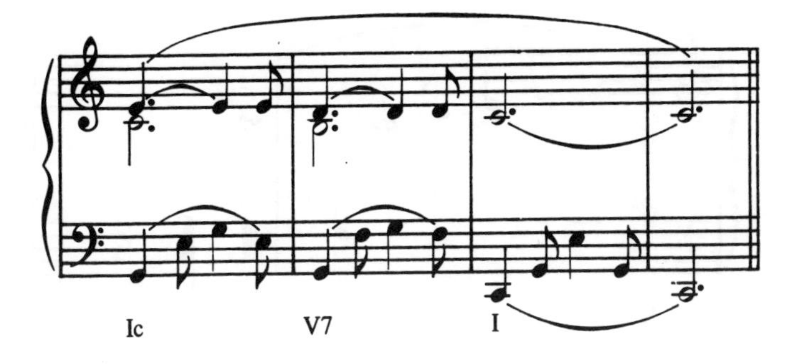

4 As a *blues*:

Example 15.24

Suggestions for further study

J. Tobin. *How to Improvise Piano Accompaniments* (Oxford University Press)
Dorothy Pilling. *Harmonisation of Melodies at the Keyboard* Books 1 to 3 (Forsyth)

Demonstration Lessons

Introduction

These lessons are designed to show you how to observe, approach, practise and listen to piano music. They include a simple piano piece, scales and *arpeggios*, and sight-reading, so that once you have grasped the 'principles' of study and practice you should be able to apply them to other pieces and situations.

Although the 'demonstration piece' is not printed in full, it is very easily obtainable, and can either be bought quite cheaply, or borrowed from the music section of a local lending library.

Lesson One: 'Melody' (Robert Schumann)
Lesson Two: Scales and Arpeggios
Lesson Three: Reading Music at Sight

Demonstration Lesson One

'Melody' (Robert Schumann)

This is the first of forty-three pieces from *Album for the Young* (Op 68), which Schumann composed in 1848. Although these pieces were intended for children to play, most of them contain technical difficulties, and all need to be played with skill and imagination. This is one of the easier pieces, which would be likely to be graded 'one' or 'two' in piano examinations. It is published by The Associated Board, Peters, Augener, etc. Any edition may be used for the purpose of this lesson, provided that it has been properly fingered and phrased. Your music dealer should be able to advise you about this.

Having obtained the piece, first number the bars *lightly* in pencil; twenty-four bars in all. It will then be easy to locate every bar which is discussed in the lesson, and the numbers can be rubbed out if the copy is on loan.

Before attempting to play anything, sit down and quietly *look through* the piece several times, carefully noting:

Clefs

Both hands are in the treble clef throughout, because in this piece the left hand plays mostly on the upper half of the keyboard.

Key

In this piece there are no sharps or flats in the key-signature, so that the music could be either in the key of C major, or in A minor. Look at the last (lowest) note in the left hand (which is *usually* the key-note); here it is C, and this piece is in the key of C major.

Example 1

Time and speed

The time-signature is $\frac{4}{4}$ (i.e. four crotchet beats in each bar, also known as *common time*, and sometimes written thus: **C**). Consider the speed at which you will *ultimately* want to play the piece. It is marked *Moderato* (at a moderate speed, not fast). If you have a metronome, and set it about 108 (i.e. 108 crotchet beats to the minute), you may feel that, having carefully considered the style and character of the music, this is about the right speed. The *exact* speed will depend on your own musical feeling and judgement, but whatever the speed you consider appropriate it will take time and patience to reach it. At first you will have to practise very slowly, always *listening* to make sure that you are playing correctly in every detail – time, phrasing, expression, pedalling, etc. It is of the utmost importance that faults should be corrected *before* they become habits.

Having considered these points, you are now ready to place the piece, and this book, on the music desk of the piano, and start to practise.

Points to watch during practice

This piece has a gentle flow throughout, and both hands must be played very smoothly, with careful attention to phrasing. You will see from the phrase marks that there are four one-bar phrases (bars 9, 10, 17 and 18); the rest of the piece consists of two-bar phrases. Start by practising the first two bars with the right hand alone. Try to keep strictly to the printed fingering unless you really feel that some modification is essential, because your hands are smaller or larger than average. The principles of fingering are dealt with more fully in Chapter 8, and you should refer to these if in doubt.

In the opening passage, which lies under the hand, the fingers are used in order when the notes are consecutive. If a note is left out, then the finger which would play the note is also left out. In Example 1, every note is fingered in order to illustrate this point. In passages exceeding a five-note span fingers may be contracted or expanded, to allow a passage to lie more easily under the hand. In a wider span of notes, the thumb may be passed under the fingers (or vice versa), as in scale playing (see page 66). The important point is to use the same fingering always, once you have decided on it.

Play this two-bar phrase quite slowly, *thinking* from the first note to the last note. To secure a perfect *legato* each sound must be carried over to the next sound without a break, one key being raised at the precise moment that the sound of the next key (which is being depressed) is heard. The fingers should remain on the surface of the keys while they are rising. It will be helpful if you can memorise the passage, so you can then watch your fingers and listen critically to what you are playing. And whatever your voice, do *sing* this phrase, as smoothly as you can, and from memory, both when you are practising, and when you are not (e.g. in the street, bath, etc.).

There is also the question of tone production. As well as positioning the fingers correctly (see Chapter 4), try to ensure that your shoulder, arm and fingers are free from unnecessary tension (see Chapter 14). Try to depress the keys by the exertion of the fingers and the weight of the arm, and not by 'striking' them; and remember that it is a waste of muscular energy to exert pressure *after* sound has been produced. On the contrary, the finger muscles should be relaxed at the moment sound begins, so that a key is held down with minimum pressure.

Now try the first two bars with the left hand. They consist almost entirely of quavers, whereas the right hand moves mostly in crotchets. However, the quavers in the first bar are not all of equal importance, those *on* the beats are 'basic' notes, whilst those *between* the beats are 'subsidiary' notes, which add movement. Thus, the first bar could be reduced to this basic pattern:

Example 2

It follows, therefore, that the 'basic' notes should be given slightly more prominence than the 'subsiduary' notes. If the damper pedal is used on each beat (as it can be throughout the piece), the general effect will therefore be:

Example 3

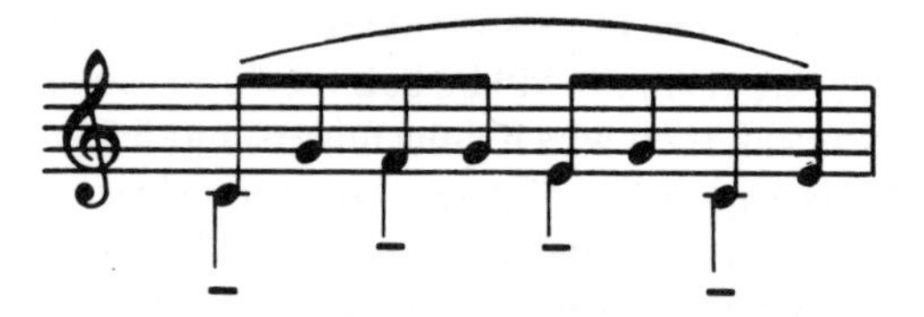

The damper pedal, if used, should be depressed immediately *after* the first note is played, then raised and depressed on the second beat. (This technique of pedalling is discussed in Chapter 12.)

Example 4

Ped. down — up down — up down — up down

The second bar for the left hand (see Example 1) also consists entirely of quavers, but the first four of these are of equal importance to those played by the right hand.

When you are reasonably satisfied with your performance of the first two bars with each hand separately, try both together. The importance of practising these two bars is apparent when you examine the structure of the piece. Bars 1 and 2 are exactly the same as bars 5 and 6, and *nearly* the same as bars 13 and 14, and bars 21 and 22 (take very careful note of the slight differences). Thus, in this twenty-four bar piece, if you can play bars 1 and 2 you should also be able to play the other six bars mentioned above. Similarly, bars 3 and 4 are the same as bars 7 and 8; and bars 9 to 12 are the same as bars 17 to 20, so that, out of twenty-four bars, no less than fourteen are the same, or nearly the same, which means that, virtually, there are only ten bars which need *individual* practice.

Now consider the tonal balance between the hands. Looking at the piece as a whole, both hands are marked with the same dynamics (*piano* in bar one, *decrescendo* in bar two, and so on), but the right hand is clearly of a different character to the left. Play each separately, and the difference should become apparent. The right hand plays a melody, and the left hand an accompaniment, so the right hand must be made more prominent than the left. In the opening bars, this could mean either that the right hand is played, say *mezzo-piano* and the left hand *piano*, or that the right hand is played *piano* and the left hand *pianissimo*. There are, of course, other possibilities, and the exact solution to the question of tonal balance is a matter for individual thought and taste. The main thing is that the performer should be able to establish a satisfactory contrast between the right hand melody and left hand accompaniment.

Next try bars 3 and 4, again with each hand separately. In bar 4 (right hand) you will probably find it easier to put the fingers over the thumb, thus:

Example 5

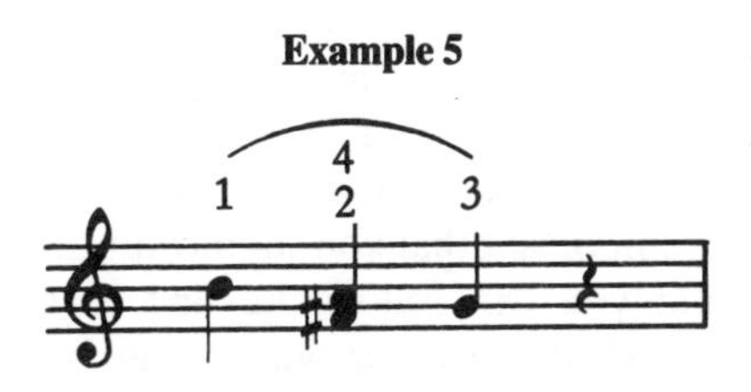

Looking again at the first four bars, you will see that although they can be considered to be made up of two two-bar phrases, the music does flow smoothly on throughout the four bars, so that you could think of it as a single four-bar phrase. Exactly how you regard the structure of these four bars does not really matter, so long as you 'think' when you play them, from the beginning of bar one to the end of bar four, and allow the music to flow along smoothly between these points. At the end of bar 4, although there is no actual break in the music, there is the feeling of temporary repose, rather like a comma in verse or prose. The fourth bar does, in fact, 'modulate'[1] for a moment, from the key of C major to the key of G major

[1] Modulate = pass from one key to another.

(returning to C major at the beginning of the fifth bar).[1] Because of this feeling of temporary repose, you could make a *very* slight break after the final note in the fourth bar. This should be done so subtly that the break is almost 'felt' rather than heard (like, perhaps, the way that a singer takes a breath between phrases). The important thing is that the rhythmic flow of the music must not be disturbed.

Observe that, in order to make the duration of the crotchet rest in bar 4 precisely one beat, the finger playing G must be raised *exactly* on the count of 4.

Bars 9 to 12 introduce a new idea made up of two one-bar phrases and one two-bar phrase. Think of the melody progressing from bar 9, reaching a climax on the first beat of bar 11, then declining. You may feel that a slight *ritardando* (slowing down) can be made during the last half bar of bar 12, returning to normal speed (*a tempo*) at the beginning of bar 13. Also at this point in bar 12, the lower moving part in the right hand is an 'imitation' of the first half of the bar and should therefore be given slight prominence.

Finally, when you have reached the stage where the fingering, notes, time, phrasing, and so on are reasonably secure, play the piece right through without stopping, noting any mistakes as you go along. Some passages will need to be isolated, and practised again on their own, but it is very important that you should appreciate the unity of the piece, so that you can follow the line of the melody and accompaniment, and the way in which one bar progresses to another.

When you are able to play the whole piece accurately, and with due regard for dynamics (soft, loud, *crescendo*) and phrasing, you can then, be gradual stages, start to increase the speed.

When you come to the final bar of this piece, you may feel that a slight *ritardando* will help to bring the music to a gentle close.

[1] Although the fourth bar could be regarded as a 'perfect' cadence in the key of G major, the musical effect is more like that of an imperfect cadence in the key of C major.

Example 6

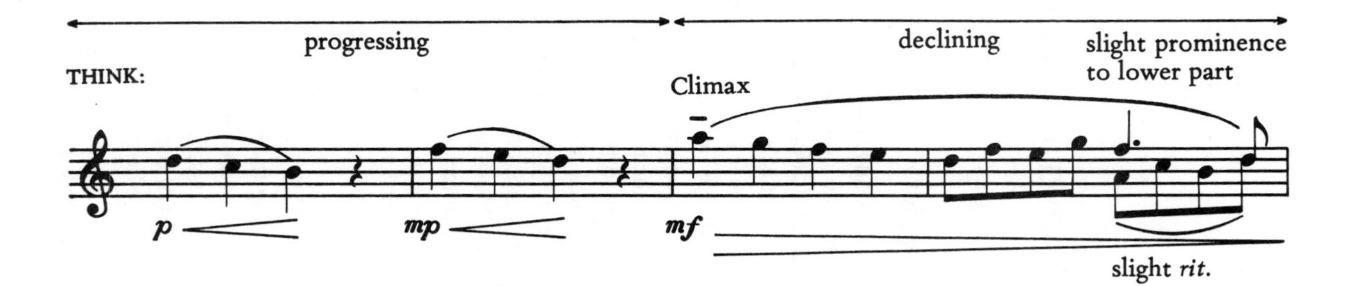
progressing
declining
slight prominence
to lower part
THINK:
Climax
p
mp
mf
slight rit.

Demonstration Lesson Two

Scales and arpeggios

Do not attempt to play any scale until you understand its structure, know from memory the notes and the fingering pattern, and can write them in your music book.

For the purpose of this lesson, we shall consider the scale of C major. From Example 6.7 (page 36) you will have seen that the C major scale has no sharps or flats in the key-signature, and that like all major scales each octave is made up of two halves, or tetrachords, each having the pattern of tone–tone–semitone, and that the two halves are joined together by a tone. Semitones therefore occur between the third and fourth, and the seventh and eighth degrees of the scale. Other adjacent notes are a tone apart. Now write in your music book one octave of the C major scale (up and down from Middle C), using Example 6.7 as a model if necessary.

Next, pick out the notes of the scale you have written on the piano keyboard with one finger. As you play, study the pattern of the notes, and continue until you can play the scale from memory.

Looking at your scale book, you will see that C major is fingered as in Example 7.

The basic pattern 123, 1̇234 (or 4321, 321) shows that when the right hand is ascending the thumb is passed under the third finger and fourth finger alternately; when descending, the third and fourth fingers are alternately passed over the thumb. The left hand fingering is the same as that of the right in reverse. Note also that the top right hand note and the bottom left hand note are both played with the fifth finger.

Real progress is only possible when notes and fingering are

Example 7

1 2 3 1 2 3 4 1 2 3 1 2 3 4 5 4 3 2 1 3 2 1 4 3 2 1 3 2 1
5 4 3 2 1 3 2 1 4 3 2 1 3 2 1 2 3 1 2 3 4 1 2 3 1 2 3 4 5

completely familiar, so start practising first with the right hand, then with the left. This can be done not only at the piano keyboard, but also with the hand resting on a desk or table at odd moments of the day. The fingering can be thought of either in terms of the basic pattern, or of the notes played by the thumb (right thumb on C and F, left thumb on G and C), remembering those top and bottom notes which are played with the fifth finger.

Even when practising away from the piano, try to visualise the notes of the scale (either on the piano keyboard, or in the scale book notation). Visual memory can usually be developed and improved by regular practice.

When you can play note and fingering patterns from memory, you should begin to study the technique of scale-playing. The object of scale practice is to produce a succession of sounds perfectly matched in quality and duration. In the early stages scales should always be played with each hand separately. If a scale is played in similar motion with both hands, weaker fingers (4th and 5th) come together, as do stronger fingers (1st, 2nd and 3rd), so it is hardly possible for the beginner to judge the tonal balance of each hand. Start, therefore, by playing first with the right hand, then with the left hand, two octaves of the C major scale.

Play the scale from memory, so that you can give your full attention to the sounds you are making, and to the movement of your fingers and arms. And, since old habits die hard, make sure that you are using the right fingering from the start (check from time to time with your scale book).

Listening carefully and critically, ask yourself whether each note is perfectly matched, and if not which are the weaker notes; whether each note is of exactly equal duration, and if not which notes are shorter than others; whether there is a true *legato* throughout, since we are trying to play the notes as smoothly as possible.

To match the tone some adjustment of the strength with which the fingers strike the keys will probably be necessary. The thumb, being rather closer to the keys than the other fingers, will need to be raised as high as they are, so that the exertion will not be less. The stronger second and third fingers may need a little restraint, and the weaker fourth and fifth fingers added strength. These are generalisations, since the relative strength of the fingers varies greatly; the ear alone must always be the final judge.

The duration of notes depends upon when and how piano keys are depressed and raised. Since we want to play *legato* one key must be depressed at the precise moment that the previous key is raised, and to ensure that successive sounds are joined together in a flowing sequence, the weight of a finger on a key (just sufficient to hold it down) must be transferred from one finger-tip to another, like a see-saw.

One of the difficulties of scale-playing is the passing of the thumb under the fingers, and of a finger over the thumb. This must be managed with the utmost smoothness and ease. Since it is easier to pass the thumb under after a black key has been played than after a white key, the C major scale, despite its easier key-signature, is technically rather more difficult than some other major scales which have the same fingering pattern (E major, for example).

The thumb, when passing under the fingers, should be moved smoothly and gradually sideways so that it arrives above the key to be played before it is required to depress it. As the thumb is tucked under the hand the arm should glide evenly along, following the movement of the hand horizontally, with no jerking or swinging of the wrist or elbow.

Since it is easier to practise small parts of a scale, the exercises in Example 13.2 (to facilitate the passage of the thumb under the fingers, and of the fingers over the thumb) should be practised and repeated as often as necessary.

The playing position of the fingers also needs to be considered. In the scale of C major, the hands should be curved so that the tips of the fingers play vertically into the centre of the keys. The thumb should be slightly bent, so that the side (with which it plays) rests on the key about as far up as the root of the nail. With scales which include black keys, modifications may be necessary.

Very slow scale practice, with each hand separately, will enable the movements of the hands to be studied closely, so that by gradually eliminating weaknesses and faults a beautifully even scale can be achieved. In detecting faults the ear must *always* be the final arbiter. Small sections of a scale which fail to satisfy the critical judgement of the ear should be isolated, so that a particular problem can be recognised and tackled accordingly. In general, it may be necessary to play a scale more slowly whenever the performance fails to satisfy.

A scale should be played at an increased speed only when it can be played slowly with the right conditions of muscular freedom and relaxation. Unnecessary tensions which may be present when a scale is played slowly are most likely to increase if it is played faster. Increases of speed should be gradual, a *very* little faster each week.

When a scale can be played effortlessly, and from memory, with each hand separately, other ways of playing it may be tried, e.g.

1 With both hands together, starting and ending on the same key-note (i.e. in contrary motion). This will often be found easier than playing with both hands in similar motion, since in many scales the fingers are used in the same order by each hand (when moving in opposite directions).
2 With both hands together in similar motion, with all kinds of dynamic variations (scales played *piano, forte,* or with *crescendo* or *diminuendo*, for example).
3 With each hand separately, and both hands together, in some of the rhythmic patterns shown in Example 13.1, page 96.
4 With each hand separately, the right hand going down and up from the highest and lowest notes of the scale on the piano; the left hand going vice versa.
5 Scales played *staccato* (each hand separately), and with various gradations of tone (*forte, piano, crescendo, diminuendo*, etc.).

Other scales can be added one by one, perhaps in the following order:

G, D, F major	A flat major	E, D minor
A, E major	B major	G, C minor
B flat, E flat major	A minor	B minor

Minor scales can be played in either melodic or harmonic form. The lower grade examinations allow the candidate to choose either form. Higher grade examinations include both forms.

Before starting to practise any new scale, study it carefully in your scale book, and make sure that you can pick out the notes on the keyboard from memory, and that you have also memorised the pattern of the fingering. Practice with closed eyes (of both scales and *arpeggios*) is a valuable way of improving tactile perception.

Arpeggios and broken chords

When playing *arpeggios* and broken chords the wrists should be slightly higher than when playing scales. When passing the thumb under the fingers in *arpeggios*, the elbows should not be raised. The lower grade examinations ask for a small number of broken chords (each hand separately), the higher grades require a number of *arpeggios*.

Before attempting to play an *arpeggio* or broken chord, pick out the notes with one finger on the keyboard, and continue until you can do so from memory.

If you are practising broken chords, you could start with C major, each hand separately (see Example 8.12(b), page 72, for fingering). After this you could practise broken chords in these keys, checking the fingering from your scale book. (Grade 2 contains the broken chords; the higher grades contain *arpeggios.)*

G, D, F major (two octaves)
A, E, D minor (two octaves)

Unevenness in broken chord playing can be helped by accenting different notes in turn (as with *arpeggio* playing) (see Example 13.4, page 99).

If you are practising *arpeggios*, you could start with C major, each hand separately (see Example 8.12(a), page 72, for fingering), and follow on with these *arpeggios*, checking the fingering from your scale book.

G, D, A, E, B, F, B flat, E flat, A flat, D flat

(major and minor, two octaves, at first with each hand separately – eventually with both hands together).

The exercises in Examples 13.3 and 13.4 will help to facilitate the smooth passage of the thumb and fingers in *arpeggio* playing, and to eliminate unevenness. As the consecutive notes in *arpeggios* (and broken chords) are farther apart than in scales, it is more difficult to obtain a completely even performance, and the relative weakness of the fourth finger needs to be carefully watched.

Demonstration Lesson Three

Reading music at sight

Sight-reading is an essential requirement for grade examinations, and for the purpose of this lesson an eight-bar piece has been written, as an example of the kind of test that might be included in Grades 2 or 3. Sight-reading is a most valuable exercise, whether or not you have an examination in mind, and the method of approach described can be applied to other pieces which are to be read at sight.

You will appreciate however that whereas, outside examination conditions, you can take as long as you like to consider a piece before you play it, or you can stop and go back, in examinations the candidate is required to read a piece at sight without stopping, and that only a limited period is allowed for looking through. (It is nevertheless extremely important that you should not start until you have a clear idea of the key, time, style, etc.).

A wrong note or two may not spoil your chances, but many examination candidates lose valuable marks because they begin to play in the wrong key or time, either because they have never acquired the habit of checking such things in advance, or because examination nerves prevent them from doing so. (For 'nerves' there is no infallible remedy, but the breathing and relaxation techniques advocated in this book may often be of considerable help.)

When sight-reading for any purpose you should choose music well within your present range, so that technical problems do not inhibit you. Also, you should try to practise sight-reading before an audience (e.g. one or two friends). Sight-reading is quite different from studying a piece. The main object of sight-reading (and, indeed, of 'performance' also) is to keep going. To do this successfully you must not only play in the right key and time, but also have an appreciation of phrasing, style, dynamics, etc. In other words, you need to develop the ability to proceed calmly, despite mistakes.

Before attempting to play Example 8, look through it slowly and carefully, trying to hear it in your mind. Note the following points:

1 Key

The absence of sharps or flats in the key-signature indicates that the key is either C major or A minor, its relative. The final chord (lowest note A) suggests that the key is A minor, and the sharpened seventh (G sharp) elsewhere in the piece tends to confirm this.

2 Time and speed

The time-signature shows that there are four crotchets to the bar. The Italian term *Allegretto* (animated but not so fast as *Allegro*) suggests a speed that is lively, but not too fast (metronome mark perhaps = c 112). Look through the whole piece and decide the speed at which you will be able to play it *accurately*. On no account try to play it faster than this. If in doubt, play it slower. Count (in your mind) four beats at the speed you have decided upon, before you start to play, and continue counting mentally throughout the piece. If you are playing it fairly slowly, you may find it helpful to sub-divide the beats by counting 'one-and, two-and, three-and, four-and'. Whatever the speed, try to keep in time, even if you make mistakes.

3 Phrasing

Carefully distinguish between *legato* notes (slurred) and *staccato* notes (with dots over or under). *Staccato* notes should normally be thought of as having half the written value (i.e. a written crotchet should be played as a quaver followed by a quaver rest). Notice that in bar 2 (fourth beat) the right hand plays *legato* and the left hand *staccato*. And in order to make the music 'flow', look upon the first four bars as a single phrase, and the last four bars as another, 'thinking' from bar one to bar four, and so on.

Example 8

4 Style

This is a most important consideration. Looking at a piece you have never seen before, how do you decide the appropriate style in which to play it? Some pieces have obvious clues: 'Alla marcia' means 'in the style of a march'. 'Tempo di Gavotta', 'Tempo di Menuetto', 'Tranquillo', 'Scherzando' indicate, respectively, the style of a Gavotte or Minuet, or a tranquil or playful style. But a piece which is marked 'Andante', 'Allegretto', 'Con moto', etc. gives an indication only of the approximate speed. The style must then be judged by looking at the phrasing, dynamics, general characteristics of the melody, harmony, etc. This is a skill which can only be acquired gradually, through experience of many different styles, and intelligent observation.

5 Dynamics

The dynamics range from *piano* to *forte*, with *mezzo-forte* in between. To obtain a noticeable contrast you will have to depress the keys gently for *piano*, more strongly for *mezzo-forte*, and more strongly still for *forte*. Make sure that the keys go down to the key-bed, and that the finger muscles are relaxed at the moment of sound, so that the keys are held down with minimum pressure. And in soft playing take care, when gently depressing a key, that the hammer reaches the string, otherwise there will be no sound. Make the *crescendo* and *decrescendo* gradually, bearing in mind that the *crescendo* during the first three beats of bar 2 can only be made with the left hand, since the right hand is sustaining a note for three beats. On the fourth beat, however, the right hand note must be increased in volume, to match the *crescendo* in the left hand.

6 Fingering

Before you start to play, have in mind the fingering you will be using, at least for the first two bars. Bars 1 and 2 should present no difficulty – each hand lies within a five-note span, so you merely have to start with the thumb, or little finger, and use the fingers in order. Bar 3 (right hand) is less straightforward. To secure a satisfactory *legato* you may find it best to pass the second finger over the thumb on the last beat. In bars 7 and 8, fingering should be chosen which will enable the sixths in the right hand to be played as smoothly as possible.

7 Pedalling

If you have sufficient experience of the principles of pedalling, the pedal may be used when sight-reading pieces like this.

8 Playing

When you are ready, take a deep, gentle breath, and as you exhale start to play (this will help to free the mind and body of unnecessary tension). While you are breathing in, count four beats in the time you have decided upon, then start to breathe out on the first beat of the music.

Example 9 suggests how this piece might be phrased, fingered and pedalled, also that a slight *ritardando* could be made in the last bar-and-a-half, to bring the piece to a gentle conclusion. This example should be closely compared with Example 8.

Example 9

Glossary of Musical Terms used in Piano Playing

All words are in Italian, unless otherwise marked.
F = French G = German I = Italian L = Latin E = English

Abbreviations

(The meaning of each word may be found by referring to that word in the Glossary.)

Accel	Accelerando	*LH (E)*	Left hand
Ad lib	Ad libitum	*Marc*	Marcato
All' 8	All' ottava	*mf*	Mezzo-forte
CD	Colla destra	*Mod*	Moderato
Coll' 8	Coll' ottava	*Mor*	Morendo
Con espress	Con espressione	*mp*	Mezzo-piano
Cres; cresc	Crescendo	*p*	Piano
CS	Colla sinistra	*Ped*	Pedal
DC	Da capo	*pp*	Pianissimo
Decres; decresc	Decrescendo	*Rall*	Rallentando
		rf; rfz; rinf	Rinforzando
Dim; dimin	Diminuendo	*RH (E)*	Right hand
		Rit; riten	Ritenuto
DS	Dal segno	*Ritard*	Ritardando
Espress	Espressivo	*sf; sfz*	Sforzando; sforzato
f	Forte		
ff	Fortissimo	*Smorz*	Smorzando
fp	Forte-piano	*Sost; sosten*	Sostenuto
fz	Forzato; forzando	*SP*	Senza pedale
		Stacc	Staccato
Leg	Legato	*Ten*	Tenuto
Legg	Leggiero	*VS*	Volto subito

Musical terms

Accelerando	Quickening the pace
Adagietto	Slightly quicker than *Adagio*
Adagio	At a slow pace (between *Andante* and *Largo*)
Adagissimo	Very slow
Ad libitum (L)	According to the performer's fancy
Affettuoso	Tender
Affrettando	Hurrying
Agitato	Agitated
Al fine	To the end (used when an earlier part of the music is to be repeated from the beginning (*Da capo*), or from the sign 𝄋 (*Dal segno*), to the end of the piece, or to the bar marked *Fine*)
All' ottavo	An octave higher
Alla	In the style of; e.g. *Alla polacca* = like a polonaise
Allegretto	Rather fast, but not so fast as *Allegro*
Allegro	Quick (between *Moderato* and *Presto*)
Amoroso	Lovingly; tenderly
Andante	At an easy pace, but less slow than *Adagio*
Andantino	Quicker than *Andante*; but in Beethoven's time sometimes slower
Animato	Animated
Appassionato	Passionately
Assai	Very
A tempo	In time (after *rall* or *accel*)
Bagatelle (F)	A trifle
Ben marcato	Well marked
Berceuse (F)	Lullaby; cradle song
Bis (L)	Twice
Bravura	Brilliance; dash
Brillante	Brilliant
Calando	Decreasing in volume or speed, or both
Cantabile	In a singing style

Colla destra	With the right hand
Coll' ottava	With the octave
Colla sinistra	With the left hand
Con anima	With life
Con brio	With vivacity, spirit
Con espressione	With expression
Con fuoco	With fire
Con grazia	With grace
Con moto	With animation
Con spirito	With spirit, life
Crescendo	Becoming louder
Da capo	From the beginning
Dal segno	From the sign (𝄋)
Decrescendo	Becoming softer
Delicato	Delicate; gentle
Diminuendo	Becoming softer
Dolce	Sweet
Espressivo	With expression
Etude (F)	Study
Fine	The end
Forte	Loud
Fortepiano	Loud, then immediately soft
Fortissimo	Very loud
Forzando; forzato	Strongly accented (see *sforzando; sforzato*)
Furioso	With fury, passion
Giocoso	Joyful
Glissando	A rapid scale played with the finger- or thumb-nail
Grandioso	Grand; magnificent
Grave	Heavy – also used to indicate a tempo slower than *Adagio*
Grazioso	Graceful
Humoreske (G)	A piece of a humorous character

Larghetto	Slow, but less slow than *Largo*
Largo	Broad; slow
Legato	Smooth
Leggiero	Light; nimble
Lentando	Gradually becoming slower
Lento	Slow
Lied (G)	Song
L'istesso tempo	The same time, or movement
Lusingando	Coaxing; caressing
Ma	But
Maestoso	Majestic
Maggiore	Major
Main droite (F)	Right hand
Main gauche (F)	Left hand
Mano destro	Right hand
Mano sinistra	Left hand
Marcato	Marked
Meno mosso	Less movement
Mezzo-forte	Moderately loud
Mezzo-piano	Moderately soft
Molto	Much
Morendo	Dying away gradually
Nobilmente	Nobly
Non troppo	Not too much
Pastorale (I or F)	In a pastoral style
Perdendosi	'Losing itself'; dying away
Pianissimo	Very soft
Piano	Soft
Più mosso	More movement
Poco	A little
Prestissimo	As quick as possible
Rallentando	Gradually becoming slower
Rinforzando	Reinforcing (a note or chord)
Ritardando	Gradually becoming slower
Risoluto	Resolute

Ritenuto	Holding back
Sans (F)	Without; e.g. *sans pédale* = without pedal
Scherzando	Playfully
Sempre	Always
Senza	Without
Sforzando; sforzato	Indicates that a note or chord so marked is to be strongly accented
Slentando	Gradually becoming slower
Smorzando	Dying away
Sostenuto	Sustained
Staccato	Short; detached
Stringendo	Increasing the speed
Svelto	Free; nimble
Tempo	Speed; time
Tempo commodo	In convenient time
Tempo primo	After a change of tempo, the pace first indicated is to be resumed
Tempo rubato	Lit. 'in robbed time'; i.e. a time in which one part of a bar is played slower or faster at the expense of the other part
Tenuto	Held; sustained
Tranquillo	Tranquil; peaceful
Transpose (E)	To read music in a higher or lower key than that in which it is written
Tre corde	Three strings (indicating the release of the left pedal)
Una corda	One string (indicating the use of the left pedal)
Vivace	Lively; brisk
Vivo	Animated
Volto subito	Turn over quickly

stretto

Index